Rising Stars

Spelling

Teacher's Guide

Spelling activities for every week

Year 1

Ione Branton

ISBN: 978-1-47187-924-1

First published in 2016 by Rising Stars UK Ltd
Rising Stars UK Ltd, part of Hodder Education Group
An Hachette UK Company
Carmelite House 50 Victoria Embankment London EC4Y 0DZ
www.risingstars-uk.com
All facts are correct at time of going to press.

Author: Ione Branton
Educational Consultant: Helen Marron
Publisher: Laura White
Illustrator: Gillian Flint c/o Bright Educational
Logo design: Julie Martin
Design: Julie Martin
Typesetting: York Publishing Solutions
Cover design: Julie Martin
Project Manager: Haremi Ltd.
Copy Editor: Haremi Ltd.
Proofreader: Haremi Ltd.

British Library Cataloguing-in-Publication Data A CIP record for this book is available from the British Library.
Printed by Ashford Colour Press Ltd.

Contents

Autumn term

Spring term

Summer term

Spelling and Phonics Strategies

National Curriculum Guidance

During year 1, teachers should build on work from the Early Years Foundation Stage, making sure that children can sound and blend unfamiliar printed words quickly and accurately using the phonic knowledge and skills that they have already learned. Teachers should also ensure that children continue to learn new grapheme-phoneme correspondences (GPCs) **and revise and consolidate those learned earlier**. The understanding that the letter(s) on the page represent the sounds in spoken words should underpin children's reading and spelling of all words. This includes common words containing unusual GPCs. The term 'common exception words' is used throughout the programmes of study for such words.

Alongside this knowledge of GPCs, children need to develop the skill of blending the sounds into words for reading and establish the habit of applying this skill whenever they encounter new words. This will be supported by practice in reading books consistent with their developing phonic knowledge and skill, and their knowledge of common exception words. At the same time they will need to hear, share and discuss a wide range of high-quality books to develop a love of reading and broaden their vocabulary.

Children should be helped to read words without overt sounding and blending after a few encounters. Those who are slow to develop this skill should have extra practice.

Spelling and Phonics Strategies:

- **Use the strategy:**

Look and Say	Cover	Write	Check
e.g. said			

- **Using syllables**
  Breaking words into syllables can support children with memory strategies (e.g. *sun-set*). Every syllable must have a vowel but 'y' can act as a vowel sound in words. For example, 'fl**y**, g**y**m and bab**y**.'
- **Split digraphs**
  Split digraphs used to be called the 'magic e,' but with synthetic phonics, the two letters make one sound rather than 'making the letter say its name.'
  For example:
  'a-e' ***same*** **'e-e'** ***these*** **'i-e'** ***time*** **'o-e'** ***home*** **'u-e'** ***clue***
  It can be helpful to give children giant letters and ask them to hold hands to show that the letters make one sound. Teachers can also draw sound buttons or lines to show that they are one sound.
- **Adjacent consonants**
  These used to be called *blends* but they are no longer taught this way, because *blending* words together is linked to segmenting words and then blending them together to read them. For example, *b-l-ow – blow*. The 'b' and 'l' are separate sounds. Be careful! Some books and resources still call these blends.
  More examples: 's-t', 'p-l', 't-r', 'n-p', 'm-p'
- **Mnemonics**
  Creating a mnemonic for 'tricky' or common exception words can help children to spell them. For example, the end of *could* – **O**h **y**ou **l**ucky **d**uck! Or *said* – **s**ally **a**lways **i**s **d**own. *People* – **p**eople **e**at **o**range **p**eel **l**ike **e**lephants.
  Encourage children to write their own mnemonic for words that they find tricky.
- **Double consonants**
  If a word has a short vowel sound followed by one consonant letter, double the last consonant letter. For example, *drop – dropped.* The short vowel sound is 'o.'
- Teachers should discuss and model the meaning of unknown words to year 1 children so that they are able to read and use their new vocabulary in writing.

	Autumn 1	Autumn 2	Spring 1	Spring 2	Summer 1	Summer 2
Week 1	**Focus:** revision of letter sounds/ names and alphabet	**Focus:** vowel digraphs 'oa/ow', as in *boat*, *own*	**Focus:** revision of digraphs from units 4–8, Autumn term	**Focus:** the /v/ sound and the /ŋ/ sound spelled 'n' before 'k'	**Focus:** revision of sounds from units 4–8, Spring term	**Focus:** adding *-ing*, as in *hunting*, *buzzing*, *jumping*
Week 2	**Focus:** revision of digraphs and segmenting skills for spelling	**Focus:** vowel digraph 'er' and 'ur', as in *her*, *turn*	**Focus:** revision of digraphs and trigraphs	**Focus:** vowel digraph 'ie' (/aɪ/) and 'ie' (/iː/), as in *lie*, *chief*	**Focus:** revision of sounds from units 9–12, Spring term	**Focus:** adding *-ed*, as in *hunted*, *buzzed*, *jumped*
Week 3	**Focus:** common exception words	**Focus:** vowel digraphs 'ai/ay' and 'oi/oy', as in *rain/play*, *oil/boy*	**Focus:** common exception words	**Focus:** split digraphs 'a-e', 'e-e', 'i-e', 'o-e', 'u-e'	**Focus:** common exception words	**Focus:** adding *-er* and *-est* to adjectives, as in *grander*, *grandest*
Week 4	**Focus:** /f/, /l/, /s/, /z/ and /k/, as in *off*, *well*, *miss*, *buzz*, *back*	**Focus:** vowel digraphs 'ee/oo'; and 'ea' (long), 'ea' (short)	**Focus:** vowel digraph 'oo' and compound words	**Focus:** graphemes 'ph' and 'wh', as in *dolphin* and *when*	**Focus:** letter string 'tch', as in *catch*, *fetch*, *kitchen*	**Focus:** adding *-er* to a verb, as in *hunter*, *buzzer*, *jumper*
Week 5	**Focus:** vowel digraphs 'ar/or', as in *car*, *born*	**Focus:** vowel trigraphs 'air', 'igh', 'ear', as in *hair*, *high*, *dear*	**Focus:** vowel digraph 'au' and 'aw', as in *author*, *saw*	**Focus:** words ending in 'y', as in *very*, *happy*, *funny*	**Focus:** adding 's' and 'es' to words, as in *cats*, *catches*	**Focus:** adding the prefix *un-*, as in *unhappy*, *undo*, *unload*
Week 6	**Focus:** vowel digraph 'ow' and 'ou', as in *now*, *out*	**Focus:** vowel digraph 'ew' and 'ue', as in *new*, *blue*	**Focus:** vowel digraph 'ir' and 'oe', as in *girl* and *toe*	**Focus:** letter strings 'ore', 'are', 'ear', as in *more*, *bare*, *pear*	**Focus:** adding 's' and 'es' to words, as in *cats*, *catches*	**Focus:** using 'k' for the /k/ sound, as in *sketch*, *kit*, *skin*

Introduction

The aim of this book is to provide some practical and exciting ways to teach spelling within the classroom. The teaching sequence closely follows the national curriculum 2014. Some of the sounds to be taught have been combined within one week's teaching to enable the entire year group's curriculum to be fully covered. Each unit (which takes up a double page within the book) shows roughly a week's worth of teaching. This might all be taught in one session or broken up over different sessions (including work at home). This is open to the teacher's discretion.

Effective spelling strategies

As part of a spelling programme different strategies need to be used to enable each individual learner to access the curriculum. Throughout the book, ideas are provided as to how to teach in a variety of styles, giving written, practical and oral activities. Learning spelling strategies is an individual process, and giving children different means by which to learn will enable them to choose an appropriate method which works for them. Effective spelling strategies should include a combination of reading and writing, together with quality teaching. This book should be used in conjunction with an individual school spelling policy to ensure that a variety of methods are used.

The primary strategies that are utilised in the teaching sequences in this book are:

- **Phonetic spelling strategies:** Awareness of phonetics is the most common method used to teach spellings, using individual phonemes representing letters together with a combination of digraphs and trigraphs representing groups of letters. Using segmenting and blending skills as part of this strategy is crucial. This is effective for most children; however awareness of common exception words that do not fit into a phonetic strategy is essential to work alongside this strategy. This strategy is the most useful basis for early spelling and is a primary focus in KS1. As children move through education, into KS2 and beyond, it is important that they have this foundation on which they can build a more extensive strategic approach.
- **Visual spelling strategy:** Some learners find this method key to successful learning. Learning how a word looks and visualising the word can be extremely effective. This can prove useful for all learners, especially with the trickier common exception words and with homophones, being able to distinguish when a word looks correct written down.
- **Mnemonics:** This method is useful in giving children a memory device by which to learn the spelling pattern of a specific word. Whilst this is useful, it does have a limitation in the number of rhymes that a child can successfully remember to be able to regularly apply this method.
- **Rule-based strategies:** Throughout the book a number of rules are provided to help give children an understanding of the theory behind spelling patterns. Understanding syllables and rules surrounding patterns can also help children learn.
- **Word-meaning strategies:** Helping children understand what words mean can support their spelling of those words. Explaining how words are derived, how prefixes and suffixes are added on to root words and how to form abbreviations and compound words, can all support confidence and accurate spelling.

Teaching a range of strategies is essential so that some of these strategies become automatic and instinctive for learners in their work.

Teaching techniques

This book aims to provide a range of teaching techniques. Children need to see confident, accurate spelling modelled using the strategies outlined above. A range of activities are provided, such as:

- **Written activities:** Look, say, cover, write, check is a well-established way of learning spellings. It has been used in a variety of ways across KS2. It is important to teach children to proofread or check their work. By giving children a modelled form of the word or sentence with which to compare their work, we can teach them to identify their errors by themselves or with support from a peer. Having done this we can further teach them to edit their spelling, thereby hopefully embedding the correct form. Encouraging children to have the confidence to attempt challenging spellings and not be afraid to try is key to progression in spelling. Dictation has also been used as a form of reviewing the quality of teaching and learning.

- **Oral activities:** It is useful for children to be able to learn spelling in oral activities. This enables words to be put into context and ensures the correct use of the words. Use of sound buttons, robot arms, chop and stretch, and other methods are helpful when learning to read and spell words. Encouraging children to be creative in sentence construction is also useful so that learned spellings are put into context whilst helping them to enjoy learning to spell.
- **Games:** These have been widely used within the book to encourage children to learn whilst they play. The games are generally followed by a different form of activity to further embed the learning. Targeted use of colouring in the identification of correct spellings and misspellings is a useful method to engage the learner and has been used in a range of ways in the activities.
- **Stories and rhymes:** These are used in the book to grab the attention of the listeners, encouraging them to spot sounds and make links with spelling patterns.

Ensuring good spelling in writing

Learners need to understand that words are made up of individual sounds (or phonemes). Once they have understood this they need to be given the opportunity to manipulate the sounds to make blended sounds and words. Only then can the process of decoding and encoding begin. For effective reading, learners need to decode using phonemic knowledge together with a range of other strategies to deal with exception words. For the process of writing, learners need to understand the converse approach – that of encoding individual phonemes. Good teaching will encourage children to manipulate sounds, practising encoding strategies whilst using the spelling principles taught. Modelling good spelling practices (e.g. within a shared or modelled writing task) is essential to encourage learners to apply the principles. Learners should also develop the use of dictionaries and other tools to check their spelling and to realise when there are word and spelling choices.

Good writers should draw on a range of spelling strategies in their work, such as:

- recalling words from memory.
- using sound-letter and phoneme knowledge to work out words.
- using knowledge of root words, prefixes and suffixes.
- using spelling rules and conventions.
- trial and error/visualisation – writing the word to check if it looks right.
- linking known words or parts of words.
- using supporting materials, such as dictionaries, phoneme mats and alphabet code charts.
- using spelling journals as an aide memoire.

This book aims to help children use good spelling in their writing using all these different strategies. At a suitable juncture after children have written a word or sentence, teachers need to encourage them to review it, proofread it and edit it if necessary. A suggested stepped approach is as follows:

- Initially ask the children to say the word they have written in its entirety.
- Secondly, the children need to be asked to decode the word they have written phonetically, if possible.
- Then ask the children to blend the sounds and say the word that they have written.
- Where the word is not phonetically decodable they need to be reminded to use one of the other strategies they have been taught (e.g. visualisation, recalling from memory, use of phoneme mats) to check if they think the word is spelled correctly.
- They should be asked if the word they have written is the word they intended, or have they created a different word.
- If they think the word is not what they intended, they should be encouraged to change it. A positive approach here is essential so as to preserve self-esteem and encourage them to try again.
- Young children can initially struggle to correct individual letters within words and it is often easier to ask them to cross out the whole word and try again. As children develop self-esteem in their ability to spell, they can be encouraged to correct letters within words.
- Finally, it is often helpful for children to ask a peer to read their work and check that what they have read is what they intended to write.

Can you find your letter partner?

Focus: revision of letter sounds/names and alphabet

You will need:

Access online resources at My Rising Stars: www.risingstars-uk.com

- Bag
- Alphabet classroom display
- Alphabet picture cards cut out
- Capital letter cards cut out
- Whiteboards and pens

In a nutshell

Teacher subject knowledge for this unit:

This week focuses on revision of the basic letter sounds and names learned in EYFS.

1 Introduce/Review

- Explain to the children that today they are going to go on a letter hunt and they are going to find all the letters of the alphabet.
- Display the alphabet (see You will need) and ask the children if they can help you by singing the alphabet song.
- After the song, briefly go through each letter sound, saying them together with the class.
- Divide the class into groups of between four and five children and give each group an equal number of picture cards from Alphabet picture cards resource (see You will need).
- Explain to the class that each picture represents one of the letters of the alphabet.
- Explain that their task is to decide in their groups what the pictures show and write the initial letter sound on the back of the picture card.
- When the groups have finished, ask them to help you make the alphabet using their pictures. Go through and ask, 'Who has got the letter "a"?' Check the picture does represent 'a' and stick it on the whiteboard. Continue with the rest of the alphabet.
- Finish by singing the alphabet song again.

2 Teach

- Remind the children that each letter can be written in lower case (small letters) and in upper case (capital letters).
- Remind the children that some letters are the same in upper case, just a bit bigger, and some letters are different. Show some examples of letters that are the same and ones that are different, e.g. *s S, v V, r R, g G*.
- Display the Alphabet resource showing both lower and upper case letters (see You will need).
- Read a word to the children and ask them to listen to the initial sound and then write the first letter of the word in a lower case letter and an upper case letter on their whiteboards. Demonstrate an example such as *car* (c, C) and *fork* (f, F).

3 Practise

- Place the capital letters from the Capital letter resource (see You will need) on the floor, facing upwards in the centre of a circle.
- Place the lower case letters from the Capital letter resource in a bag.
- Pass the bag around the circle while saying the following rhyme:

  Looking for some letters
  In the alphabet
  Let's stop and match the letter
  Is it on the carpet?

- When the rhyme has finished, ask the child holding the bag to pick one of the cards. They should then show the class, sound out the letter and find the matching capital letter on the floor. Place the lower case and capital letter together and continue to match the other cards.
- While doing this, check that the children know and can say both the phonetic sound and the letter names.

Challenge!

Use the Spelling Fox Challenge: Can you find your letter partner? to kick off or consolidate the learning. The children must help the Spelling Fox find the correct answers! Access online via My Rising Stars.

4 Apply

Activity 1: Find my partners

- Give each child a card with either a lower case letter, upper case letter (from Capital letter resource) or a picture (Alphabet picture card resource) at random. Ask the children to space themselves out around the room.
- Tell the children that their challenge today is to match each picture with its lower case letter and its upper case letter.
- Demonstrate by choosing a child, sounding out the letter and then sounding out the child's letter using a picture, e.g. *jelly, j.*
- Tell the children to sit on the floor in a circle in their threes when they have found their linking sound.
- When all the children have found their groups, go around the circle sounding out the letters and saying the words from the pictures.
- Repeat the activity, giving children different letters.

Activity 2: Clap, clap, turn around

- Tell the children that you are now going to play a game using their whiteboards and pens.
- Ask the class to stand in a circle with their whiteboards and pens on the floor in front of them.
- Say the following rhyme with actions and then ask the children to quickly sit down and write the sound.

  Clap, clap, turn around,
  I'm going to tell you a letter name and I want you to write it down.
  The letter is '…'.

- Once the children have written the letter in both lower and upper case, ask them to show you their whiteboards on the count of three.

5 Review

- Give small groups of children the cut-out cards from Capital letter resource.
- Ask the children to muddle up the cards and turn them face down.
- Ask the children to take it in turns to choose a card and turn it over.
- Demonstrate choosing a card and asking the children to identify if it is a lower case letter or an upper case letter.
- If the letter card is lower case, ask the children to write the same letter but as upper case. Repeat this to demonstrate that if the letter is upper case they should write a lower case letter.
- Once they have written the letters they should check the formation of their letter using an alphabet display on the whiteboard.
- The group should then use this letter to say some words that start with this letter sound.
- Ask the children to continue this in groups, taking turns to choose a letter.

Can you reach the King?

Focus: revision of digraphs and segmenting skills for spelling

You will need:

Access online resources at My Rising Stars: www.risingstars-uk.com

- Soft ball
- Whiteboards and pens
- Reach the King playing board per pair
- Dice and counters
- Bubble challenge resource per child
- Colouring pencils

In a nutshell

Teacher subject knowledge for this unit:

This week focuses on the revision of digraphs and segmenting skills learned in EYFS.

1 Introduce/Review

Activity 1: Quick spell

- Ask the class to stand in a circle.
- Explain that this is a quick game and that if the children are not quick they will break up the word. Explain that the class challenge is to be quick to keep the flow of the word.
- Explain that you are going to give the class a word and their challenge is to spell it using the sounds. Demonstrate doing this with *leg*, 'l-e-g'.
- Now explain that when they are thrown the ball they need to say the next sound in the word. Demonstrate this by throwing the ball to different children and asking them to sound out the word 'c-a-p', saying one letter each.
- When the word is finished the whole class should say the whole word *cap*.
- Explain that if children are too slow then the word being spelled out becomes too slow and it may need to be restarted so that it flows clearly.
- Give the children a range of CVC words and then include words using the 'ck', 'ch', 'sh', 'th', 'ng' and 'qu' digraphs (*tick, chick, chop, shop, mash, thing, ring, quick, queen*).

2 Teach

- Write the revision digraphs on the whiteboard – 'ck', 'ch', 'sh', 'th', 'ng' and 'qu'.
- Remind the children that these sounds are called digraphs and that they are two phonemes that together make an individual sound.
- Ask the children to say these sounds and ask them to practise writing them on their whiteboards.
- Explain that some of the words they spelled out in the previous session used these digraphs, and their challenge is to help you spell them.
- Read the word *chop* and ask the children to help you sound it out and write it on the whiteboard. Underline the digraph 'ch'.
- When the children sound out the words, remind them to use the school strategy for segmenting words (robot arms, chop and stretch, sound buttons etc.).
- Repeat this with the words *shop*, *ring* and *path*, making sure that the children are identifying the digraph sounds.

3 Practise

Activity 2: Clap, clap, turn around

- Tell the children that you are now going to play a game using their whiteboards and pens.
- Ask the class to stand in a circle with their whiteboards and pens on the floor in front of them.
- Say the following rhyme with actions and then ask the children to quickly sit down and write the word.

Clap, clap, turn around,
I'm going to tell you a word and I want you to write it down.
The word is '…'.

> **Challenge!**
> Use the Spelling Fox Challenge: Can you reach the King? to kick off or consolidate the learning. The children must help the Spelling Fox find the correct answers! Access online via My Rising Stars.

- Select a range of CVC and CVCC words, e.g. *pig, cup, kick, ring, tank.*
- Once the children have written the word, ask them to show you their whiteboards on the count of three.

4 Apply

Activity 3: Reach the King

- Give pairs of children the Reach the King playing board resource and a dice (see You will need).
- Explain that they need to help reach the king, who is at the end of the board.
- Demonstrate rolling the dice and moving a counter the correct number of squares from the start of the board.
- Tell the children that they then need to say the word correctly, cover it over and then write it correctly. Demonstrate this and ask a child to check your spelling.
- Explain to the children that if they get the word correct they can stay where they are, but if they get it wrong they must move back to the square they started their turn on.
- Pairs of children play the game, continuing until one player reaches the king.
- This activity can be repeated with children landing on different squares.

Activity 4: Colour the sounds

- Show the children the Bubble challenge resource (see You will need).
- Tell the children that all of the words in the bubbles use one of the sounds that they are revising this week.
- Tell them that their challenge is to find each sound and to colour each one in the correct colour.
- Ask the children to take a yellow crayon and find and colour all the words that use a 'ch' sound. Then ask the children to take a brown crayon and colour all the words using the 'ck' sound.
- Once the children are familiar with the task, show them the key at the bottom of the sheet. Ask them to now colour the remaining sounds in the correct colours according to the key.
- Give the children time to complete the sound identification colouring.
- Ask the class to compare the patterns they have made. If coloured correctly, they should see two flowers in the pattern. Check that they are all the same, and if there are any differences then ask the class to check which one of them is correct.

5 Review

- Dictate the following phrases for the class to write in their spelling journals.
- Before writing, ensure that the children orally rehearse the phrase.

  Fish and chips
  Quick king
  This duck
  Ring shop
  Thin chap

Can you write it right?

Focus: common exception words

You will need:

Access online resources at My Rising Stars: www.risingstars-uk.com

- Exception cards cut out
- Whiteboards and pens
- Bag

In a nutshell

Teacher subject knowledge for this unit:

This week focuses on words which are not phonetically decodable. Generally the grapheme-phoneme correspondences do not fit in with what has been taught so far. Children need to be taught to learn these words in different ways and to become familiar with them by sight.

Word list

the	he	be	says
I	a	she	me
today	do	of	we
they	said	to	

1 Introduce/Review

- Write the word *the* on the whiteboard. Try sounding it out and then explain that this word cannot be sounded out.
- Explain that this week they are looking at words that are different to how they sound and that these words are called 'exceptions'.
- Show the letters 'a' and 'i' and explain that there are two ways of saying these: as phoneme sounds, or as we would normally say them in a sentence. For example, 'a' as in *apple* or 'a' as in *around*, 'i' as in *indigo* or 'i' as in *island*.
- Put the cut-out cards from Exception cards (see You will need) into a bag and have the children sit in a circle.
- Tell the children that they are going to go on an 'exception word hunt'. Explain that these words have become muddled up with words that are easy to sound out phonetically and that their task is to sort them out and find the exception words.
- Demonstrate selecting a card without looking and then sounding it out. Ask the children whether it makes sense. If it does, then it is not an exception word and can be kept in a separate pile. If it is an exception word, then place the card on the floor in the middle of the circle.
- Pass the bag around the circle and as a class all say the following chant:

  We are going on a word hunt.
  Can we find an exception word?
  Let's stop and look around.
  Have we found a tricky one?

  At the end of the rhyme the child holding the bag selects a card and continues as modelled.
- Continue until the class has sorted all the cards. Read through the exception word cards in the middle of the circle for reinforcement.
- Keep the exception cards that have been found for the next session.

2 Teach

- Remind the children of the exception words from the previous session and display the words that the class sorted.
- Remind the children that the words they are learning this week cannot be sounded out and blended normally.
- Ask the class to help sound out the word *today* and blend it, demonstrating that it is an exception word. Explain how to say it properly.
- Ask the children to take a minute to look at the word and try to learn it.

> **Challenge!**
> Use the Spelling Fox Challenge: Can you write it right? to kick off or consolidate the learning. The children must help the Spelling Fox find the correct answers! Access online via My Rising Stars.

- Now ask the children to write this word on their whiteboards without looking.
- Check the spelling of their work.
- Ask the children to talk to a partner and explain how they learned this word. Highlight the different ways the children learned the word and remind the class that there are many different ways to learn, e.g. the children might learn by remembering the word visually or by remembering the way it is phonetically sounded out.
- Repeat for *they* and *said*.
- Write the group of words *be, me, he, she* and *we* on the whiteboard and explain how these words use a similar pattern, changing one letter each time.

3 Practise

- Turn the remaining cards from the word list from the Exception cards resource upside down on the floor.
- Ask a child to choose a card. Ask the child to try to say the word, giving support if necessary. The child then shows the rest of the class, who repeat the word.
- The children now individually choose one of the learning methods (see *Teach* session) to learn the word.
- The class writes the word on their whiteboard and shows it for checking.
- Repeat for the rest of the words.

4 Apply

Activity 1: Find the exception

- Give pairs of children the cut-out Exception cards (see You will need).
- Spread the cards face up on the floor or table so that they are visible.
- Demonstrate reading a word aloud from one of the cards without indicating which card it is. Ask a partner to find the card that you have read.
- Explain to the class that they should play 'find the exception' in their pairs. When they have found the card, they can keep it if it is correct.
- Play until all the cards have been claimed. The child with the most cards wins the game.
- Children can swap partners and replay the game.

Activity 2: Write it right

- Tell the children that today they are going to try to write the exception words right (correctly) in playing the game 'Write it right'.
- Demonstrate turning the Exception cards face down on the floor or table.
- One child chooses a card and reads what it says without showing their partner.
- Their partner now needs to write the word on their whiteboard.
- They show their whiteboard and the first child checks that the word is spelled correctly.
- If it is correct then it can be kept by the child who has written the word. If it is incorrect then it is placed back down with the rest of the cards.
- The game continues until all the cards have been claimed.

5 Review

- Give pairs of children the cut-out Exception cards.
- The pairs should spread the cards out face up in front of them. Ask them to orally compose a sentence that uses at least one of the cards. Initially ask the children to share some of their sentences with the class.
- Once they have composed a sentence using one of the words, they can 'collect' the card from the table and continue to compose a sentence using a different word(s).
- Continue composing sentences until all the words have been used by the pair.

Can you add the ending?

Focus: /f/, /l/, /s/, /z/ and /k/, as in *off, well, miss, buzz, back*

You will need:

Access online resources at My Rising Stars: www.risingstars-uk.com

- Sorting sound table per group
- Word cards cut out
- Find the ending resource per child

In a nutshell

Teacher subject knowledge for this unit:

The /f/, /l/, /s/, /z/ and /k/ sounds are usually spelled as 'ff', 'll', 'ss', 'zz' and 'ck' if they come straight after a single vowel letter in short words. Exceptions: *if, pal, us, bus, yes*.

Word list

/f/	/l/	/s/	/z/	/k/
off	well	miss	buzz	back
puff	fell	pass	fuzz	pack
stuff	smell	press	fizz	smack
stiff	tell	fuss	jazz	neck
cliff	tall	hiss	whizz	pick
fluff	will	class		stick
	doll	cross		clock
	ball	kiss		duck
	fall	dress		luck

1 Introduce/Review

- Tell the children that this week they are learning some different sounds that often come at the end of words.
- Say the /f/ sound and ask the class to repeat it, checking for correct pronunciation. Repeat with /l/, /s/, /z/ and /k/ sounds.
- Write the word *off* on the whiteboard and use sound buttons to show the digraph 'ff' at the end of the word. Repeat for *well, miss, buzz* and *back*, underlining the digraph at the end of each.
- Tell the children that you have some words that use these sounds but they have become a bit muddled and you need the children's help to sort them out into the correct sounds.
- Draw five columns on the whiteboard with a different digraph ending as a heading for each. Alternatively, the Sorting sound table resource (see You will need) could be used for this purpose.
- Demonstrate choosing one word (e.g. *dress*), underlining the digraph ending ('ss') and then placing it in a column for words ending 'ss'.
- Give small groups of children the Sorting sound table resource and the cut-out Word cards (see You will need) and ask them to underline the digraph ending, read the word and then to sort the cards into the same digraph ending sounds.
- Take feedback from the groups and check for accurate sorting of the words.

2 Teach

- Show one of the word cards from the previous session (e.g. *fell*) and sound it out phonetically 'f-e-l-l'. Try to blend it repeating the /l/ sound twice. Ask the children if it sounded correct and ask them how you should say the word.
- Explain that the two /l/ sounds at the end of the word blend to make a digraph so they do not need to be said individually.
- Repeat the exercise for *kiss* and *pick*.
- Explain that we need to double the letter at the end when we have a short 'a', 'e', 'i', 'o' or 'u'. Tell the children that these are special letters called vowels and write them on the whiteboard.

> **Challenge!**
> Use the Spelling Fox Challenge: Can you add the ending? to kick off or consolidate the learning. The children must help the Spelling Fox find the correct answers! Access online via My Rising Stars.

- Ask the class to help you write *dress* on the whiteboard. Write 'd-r-e' and highlight the short /e/ sound and ask the class to help you finish the word with 'ss'.
- Repeat with the words *whizz* and *duck*.

3 Practise

- Ask the children to sit in a circle and give each of them a whiteboard and pen.
- Spread the cut-out Word cards face down on the floor in the middle of the circle.
- Ask a child to choose a card and, without showing the rest of the class, read it out. Encourage the child to sound it out first and then blend the sounds together.
- Ask the rest of the class to write the word on their whiteboards.
- When all the children have finished writing, the child holding the word card shows the class and checks the children's spelling. Ask any children who have not spelled the word correctly to write it again, with support from the children who spelled it correctly and are sitting nearby.
- Continue choosing different children to select a card.

4 Apply

Activity 1: Find my family

- Give each child a cut-out Word card and tell them to keep it secret from anyone else.
- Ask the children to make sure that they know what their card says and give support if necessary.
- Ask the children to stand up and space themselves around the classroom.
- Explain to the children that their challenge is to find the other three children that have words that use the same digraph ending so that they have a family of four together.
- Tell the children that they need to move around the class and say their word to another child. Explain that they need to say their word very carefully and listen very carefully to find their families, especially if they have a /s/ or /z/ ending, which are very similar.
- Explain that once they have found another child with the same ending they need to stay together and search together for another matching digraph ending.
- Once the children are sitting in their families, ask them to show their cards and to check that all their words do end in the same digraph.

Activity 2: Silent families

- Tell the class that they are going to play 'Find my family' (Activity 1) but with a difference!
- Explain that this time the children must choose their own word and write it on a whiteboard.
- They must then play the game in a similar way but without any talking. They need to show their whiteboard to another child and read each other's words silently in their heads to find their families.
- Explain to the class that the families could be different sizes so they need to keep checking.
- Once they have found their family they should all read aloud their words to check the digraph sound.

5 Review

- Show the children the Find the ending resource (see You will need).
- Explain that the words on the sheet have lost their endings and the class needs to help find the correct digraph to finish the words.
- Explain that there is a picture to help them and they should use the bubble prompt on the sheet to try different digraphs to find which one makes sense. Demonstrate this trial and error approach with 'pre', 'ff','ll' and 'ss' to make *press*.
- When the children have finished, ask them in pairs to orally compose sentences that use each word.

Can you help the horse find the corn?

Focus: vowel digraphs 'ar/or', as in *car*, *born*

You will need:

Access online resources at My Rising Stars: www.risingstars-uk.com

- 'ar/or' poems for display
- 'ar/or' resource for display
- Help the horse get to the corn playing board per pair
- Counters
- Whiteboards and pens

In a nutshell

Teacher subject knowledge for this unit:

If you can hear the /ar/ sound in a word, it is almost always spelled 'ar'. The most common spelling of the /or/ sound is 'or'.

Word list

ar		or	
car	hard	for	corn
start	bark	short	horn
park	dark	born	torn
arm	harm	horse	sport
garden	sharp	morning	porch
far	arch	cork	torch
jar	army		
scar	artist		

1 Introduce/Review

- Tell the children that they have two new sounds to learn this week and that you have some silly rhymes to read them that use these sounds.
- Read 'The Park in the Dark' from the 'ar/or' poems resource (see You will need) and ask the children if they can hear any repeated sounds.
- Take feedback from the class as to what sound they could hear. The poem may need to be repeated with the sound slightly stressed.
- Once the children have identified the sound, re-read the poem and ask the children to raise their hand when they hear a word that uses this sound. At each word stop and ask the children to repeat the word with you.
- The poem could also be displayed on the whiteboard and the /ar/ words highlighted.
- Repeat this for the second poem, 'Short Night', from the 'ar/or' poems resource, but remind the children that they are listening for a different sound in this poem.
- Display the highlighted poems on the working wall.

2 Teach

- Ask the children to recall the two sounds that they are learning this week from the poems read in the previous session.
- Write 'ar' and 'or' on the whiteboard. Sound out each digraph and check that they know how to say both sounds.
- Explain that there are different ways of writing and saying these two sounds, but that if you can hear the /ar/ it is almost always spelled 'ar'. Explain that the 'or' spelling is also the most common for the /or/ sound.
- Ask the children to help you write *park* on the whiteboard, underlining the digraph 'ar'. Repeat this for *bark*, *horn* and *torch*.

Challenge!

Use the Spelling Fox Challenge: Can you help the horse find the corn? to kick off or consolidate the learning. The children must help the Spelling Fox find the correct answers! Access online via My Rising Stars.

3 Practise

- Show the class the 'ar/or' resource (see You will need) on the whiteboard.
- Explain that they need to use either the /ar/ sound or the /or/ sound to complete each word. Demonstrate testing the first example with /ar/ and /or/ to decide which makes more sense.
- Ask the children to write the rest of the words on their whiteboards or in their spelling journals using the correct digraph.
- Go through the words with the class and check for accurate spelling. Clarify understanding of any unfamiliar words.

4 Apply

Activity 1: Help the horse get to the corn

- Show the children the playing board Help the horse get to the corn (see You will need).
- Explain that they will play in pairs, one of them being the /or/ sound and one of them being the /ar/ sound.
- Demonstrate choosing a word from the first line and sounding it out, moving your counter to that word when it is said correctly. Explain that the aim is to get their counter to the top of the board and that they can only move their counter on to a word that they can say correctly.
- Take turns, each following the path of the words with their given sounds. Explain that they can only move up, down or adjacent, not diagonal, and that sometimes they might need to go sideways to be able to get to the top (the corn).
- Give the children counters and let them play the game.
- When finished they can swap sounds and replay the game.

Activity 2: Claim the corn for the horse

- Give pairs of children the Help the horse get to the corn playing board.
- Explain to the children that this time they are going to play the game differently. Explain that each of the words is a piece of corn and their challenge is to claim more corn for their horse than their partner.
- Demonstrate choosing a word and saying it. Ask the class to act as your partner and if they agree that you have said the word correctly then you can colour the word to claim it.
- Remind the children to choose a different colour from their partner.
- Continue until all the words have been claimed, and then count the words to decide whose horse has the most corn and who has won the game. (Counters can also be used to claim the corn instead of colouring so that the boards can be reused.)

5 Review

- Dictate the following sentences to the class:

  I park the car.
  The horse had the corn.
  We will start sport.
  In the morning it is not dark.

- Ask the children to write the sentences in their spelling journals.

Can you make four-in-a-row?

Focus: vowel digraph 'ow' and 'ou', as in *now, out*

You will need:

Access online resources at My Rising Stars: www.risingstars-uk.com

- 'ow/ou' picture cards cut out
- Bag
- 'ow/ou' four-in-a-row playing board per pair
- Counters
- Whiteboards and pens

In a nutshell

Teacher subject knowledge for this unit:

When the 'ow' precedes an 'n' or 'l' it is usually spelled 'ow', e.g. *town, owl.*
The common exception word that does not follow this pattern is *you* and this needs to be explained to the children.

Word list

ow		ou	
now	howl	out	sound
how	growl	about	aloud
brown	prowl	mouth	round
down	cow	around	
town	clown		
owl	crown		
vow			

1 Introduce/Review

- Tell the children that they are learning the 'ow' sound and that their task this week is to find some words that use this sound.
- Ask the children to talk to a partner and see if they can come up with some words that use this sound.
- Take verbal feedback from the class and for each word stress the 'ow' sound.
- Ask the class to sit in a circle. Place the cut-out pictures from the 'ow/ou' picture cards resource (see You will need) into a bag. Explain to the children that all the pictures in the bag represent a word that uses the 'ow' sound.
- Explain that the bag will be passed around the circle whilst the following rhyme is being said:

  We are learning how to spell.
  We can do it very well.
  We are looking for a sound.
  Is this the word in which it's found?

- When the rhyme finishes the child holding the bag takes one of the pictures out of the bag.
- This child, together with help from the two children either side, needs to try to decide what word it might be that uses the 'ow' sound. If they do not get it right, the rest of the class and teacher help to find the 'ow' sound.

2 Teach

- Remind children of the 'ow' sound that they are learning this week.
- Explain that the 'ow' sound can be made using different letters.
- Write the words *now* and *out* on the whiteboard and underline the 'ow' and 'ou' digraphs. Explain that the words they are learning this week will have one of these two digraphs for the 'ow' sound.
- Tell the children that there is one commonly used word which ends in 'ou' which is *you* and that this word does not have the 'ow' sound.
- Tell the children that when the 'ow' sound comes before an 'n' or 'l' it usually uses the 'ow' spelling, e.g. *howl, crown.*

Challenge!

Use the Spelling Fox Challenge: Can you make four-in-a-row? to kick off or consolidate the learning. The children must help the Spelling Fox find the correct answers! Access online via My Rising Stars.

3 Practise

Activity 1: Find the 'ow' and 'ou'

- Show the children the four-in-a-row game board from the 'ow/ou' four-in-a-row resource (see You will need).
- Explain that on the board all the words have the 'ow' sound in them, but that some of them use 'ow' and some use 'ou'.
- Ask the children to work in pairs to sound out the words and practise saying them. Ask them to then decide if the word uses 'ow' or 'ou'.
- Ask them to colour the 'ow' words one colour and the 'ou' words another colour.
- After the children have completed the task, ask the class if they have found a hidden letter and highlight that the 'ou' sound words should make a circular shape in the grid.
- Keep the game boards for use in Activity 2 and 3.

4 Apply

Activity 2: Four-in-a-row

- Give the children the 'ow/ou' four-in-a-row game board from the 'Practise' session.
- Remind the children that the coloured squares will help them remember which 'ow' sound is used in each word.
- Explain that the idea of the game is to connect four words in a row, either horizontally, vertically or diagonally.
- Play the game with a child at the front of the class. Demonstrate choosing a word and saying it correctly to claim the word.
- Children have different coloured counters to place on the words that they have successfully claimed.
- Explain that if they do not get the word right the other player has a chance to steal the word by saying it correctly.

Activity 3: Four-in-a-row sentences

- This game is played exactly as in Activity 2, but this time the children need to orally compose a sentence using the word they choose.
- The other player should check to make sure that it makes sense and then the first player can claim the word.
- Take turns to play the game and continue until a player has claimed 'four-in-a-row'.
- Swap partners and replay the game.

5 Review

- Give the children the 'ow/ou' four-in-a-row game board from the 'Practise' session and some counters.
- Demonstrate choosing any word at random, sounding it out using the 'ow/ou' digraph, then covering it over with a counter.
- Ask a child to be your partner and to write this word on their whiteboard while it is hidden by the counter.
- Now uncover the word and demonstrate checking it together with your partner. If it is correct then the child who has written the word keeps the counter.
- Ask the children to continue this game in pairs and at the end of the lesson reward the children with the most counters.

Can you find a happy goat and a kindly crow?

Focus: vowel digraphs ‘oa/ow’, as in *boat*, *own*

You will need:

Access online resources at My Rising Stars: www.risingstars-uk.com

- A Happy Goat and a Kindly Crow poem for display
- ‘oa/ow’ cards cut out per pair
- Whiteboards and pens

In a nutshell

Teacher subject knowledge for this unit:

The digraph ‘oa’ is very rare at the end of an English word.

Word list

oa		ow	
boat	coal	own	below
coat	goal	blow	bowl
road	foal	snow	crow
goat	soap	grow	mow
soak	roast	show	show
croak	toast	arrow	throw
cloak	float	flow	yellow

1 Introduce/Review

- Tell the children that you are going to read a short poem called ‘A Happy Goat and a Kindly Crow’. Tell them that many of the words in the poem use the same sound and ask whether they can spot it as you read the passage.
- Read the title again and ask if they can already spot the sound that it might be.
- Read the first verse of ‘A Happy Goat and a Kindly Crow’ (see You will need).
- Take answers from the children as to what the sound might be.
- Read the next verse and again ask what the sound might be. Finish the poem.
- Explain that the sound they are looking at this week is the ‘oa/ow’ sound.
- Read the passage again and ask the children to put their thumbs up when they hear a word with the ‘oa/ow’ sound.
- Show the passage on the whiteboard and, as you read, ask children to come and highlight the words with the ‘oa/ow’ sounds.
- Ask the children what they notice about the first two verses of the poem and the words that they have highlighted (each verse uses a different spelling of the ‘oa/ow’ sound).
- Display the highlighted passage on the working wall.

2 Teach

- Write up ‘oa’ and ‘ow’ on the whiteboard.
- Ask the class to say each of these sounds and explain that they are said in exactly the same way.
- Explain that the digraph used depends on the word and that this week they will be learning some of the words that use this sound.
- Display the highlighted poem from the previous session.
- Explain that all the highlighted words in the first verse use the ‘oa’ spelling. Say the words as a class and then in pairs, sounding them out if necessary.
- Explain that all the highlighted words in the second verse use the ‘ow’ spelling. Say the words as a class and then in pairs, sounding them out if necessary.
- Look at the final verse and explain that the highlighted words here use a mixture of the two spellings.

Challenge!

Use the Spelling Fox Challenge: Can you find a happy goat and a kindly crow? to kick off or consolidate the learning. The children must help the Spelling Fox find the correct answers! Access online via My Rising Stars.

3 Practise

- Give pairs of children the cut-out 'oa/ow' cards from the resources (see You will need).
- Demonstrate sounding out and blending a word.
- Then demonstrate sorting the words into two piles, one pile with the label 'oa' and one pile with the label 'ow'.
- When the children have sorted their words, in pairs they can check each other's work. Encourage them to read the words automatically where possible.

4 Apply

Activity 1: Find the match

- Give small groups of children two copies of the cut-out 'oa/ow' cards.
- Children turn them over and spread them out on the table or floor.
- Demonstrate how to play the game by choosing and turning over two cards. The player needs to then say both words aloud. The other players need to check the word is said correctly. If they match then the player can keep the pair and have another go.
- Explain that if they do not match then the player should turn them back over and place them in their original positions. The next player then has a turn.
- Encourage the children to remember where the words were placed and to find them again when they have a word that matches.

Activity 2: Snap that word

- Combine three or four groups of cut-out cards from the 'oa/ow' card resource used in Activity 1. Deal the cards out between three and five players.
- Each player turns over a card at the same time. If the cards match, the first player to say 'snap' wins the cards.
- Continue to play until all the cards have been won.

5 Review

- Dictate the following sentences to the class:

  The snow can blow in the wind.
  She sat in a boat with a float.
  Today I will show you my yellow coat.
  When I grow up I will go out on my own.
- Ask the children to write the sentences in their spelling journals.

Can you swap it?

Focus: vowel digraph 'er' and 'ur', as in *her, turn*

You will need:

Access online resources at My Rising Stars: www.risingstars-uk.com

- 'er/ur' picture cards cut out
- Swap it! word cards cut out twice
- Make a word resource per child
- Music

In a nutshell

Teacher subject knowledge for this unit:

The 'er' sound within a word can be stressed (i.e. you can hear the 'er' sound in the word), as in *her or verb*, or it can be unstressed, as in *sister* or *under*.

Word list

er		ur	
stressed	**unstressed**	turn	fur
her	under	hurt	blur
term	summer	church	curl
verb	winter	burst	surf
person	sister	Thursday	return
fern		Saturday	burn
term			

1 Introduce/Review

- Sit the class in a circle and spread out the picture cards from the 'er/ur' resource (see You will need) face down in the middle.
- Tell the children that the sound they are learning this week is in each of the words that are represented by the pictures on the floor.
- Ask a child to choose a picture and say what they think it is. The rest of the class can help to say what they think the picture might be. At this point you might have several suggestions, e.g. *winter, cold, snow*.
- Ask another child to choose a different picture and take suggestions about what the word might be. Continue doing this and support children to make links with the 'er/ur' sound in each word.
- Go through all the pictures and ensure that all children know the 'er/ur' word that the picture represents.

2 Teach

- Recap the words from the picture cards and remind the children that this week they are learning the 'er' sound.
- Write 'er' on the whiteboard and ask the children to help you say this digraph. Check for correct pronunciation.
- Repeat for 'ur' and highlight that this is pronounced the same way.
- Ask the children to help you write *her, term* and *fern*, underlining the digraph 'er' each time. Check the children understand all of these words.
- Repeat this with *turn, blur* and *curl*.
- Show the word *Thursday* and practise sounding this out and writing it as a class. Repeat for *Saturday*.

3 Practise

- Divide the pictures from the 'er/ur' picture card resource into two groups – those using the 'er' spelling and those using 'ur' spellings.
- Divide the class into two groups and give each group a different set of pictures. Ensure each group knows which spelling of 'er/ur' they have been given.

Challenge!
Use the Spelling Fox Challenge: Can you swap it? to kick off or consolidate the learning. The children must help the Spelling Fox find the correct answers! Access online via My Rising Stars.

- Each group should have their pictures visible. One child should choose a picture and tell the group what word it represents. The whole group should sound out the word and then write the word on their whiteboards or in their spelling journals.
- The child who chose the card should then check their spelling with the teacher and the rest of the group should use this child's work to check their work, correcting it if necessary.
- The children should take it in turns to choose cards and when the words from all the cards have been written the groups can swap cards.

4 Apply

Activity 1: Swap it!

- Show the children the word cards from the Swap it! resource (see You will need) and check for understanding.
- Ask the children to sit in a circle. Pass the word cards around so each child has one and the remaining cards are in a pile in the middle of the circle. Ensure that there are two copies of each word.
- Ask the children to tell their partner what their word says. Listen for any errors and correct if necessary.
- Play some music and pass the cards around the circle. Encourage the children to keep passing the words whilst the music is playing. When the music stops the children keep the card they are holding.
- Ask the children to tell their partner what the word they are holding says. Listen for any errors and correct if necessary.
- Choose a child to say their word aloud.
- The child who has the same word shouts "Swap it". This second child takes a new card from the pack and reads this word out. The child with the same card shouts "Swap it" and takes a new card, and so the game continues.
- If two children both have the same word, they both 'Swap it' and the first to shout is the child who reads their new word. If no child has the same word the music is restarted and the game continues from the start.
- 'Swap it' three times then restart the music and move the cards around the circle. Repeat the activity.

Activity 2: Make a word

- Show the children the Make a word resource (see You will need). Explain that some of the letters have become jumbled and they need to sort them out to make a word which uses the 'er/ur' sound.
- Tell them each '_' represents one letter of the word.
- Remind them to sound out the word carefully and to check that their word makes sense when they have filled in the letters.
- Demonstrate completing the first word.
- Ask the children to complete the word jumble independently.
- Take feedback from the class and check for accurate spelling.

5 Review

Activity 3: Oral composition

- Give pairs of children some of the word cards from the Swap it! resource.
- Ask the pairs to choose at least one card and orally compose a sentence that uses this word.
- Once the pairs have composed a sentence they should share it with another pair. This second pair needs to then say which word in their sentence uses the 'er' sound and whether it uses the 'er' spelling or the 'ur' spelling. The pairs then swap roles and listen to the other composed sentence.
- Repeat using a different word and with different pairs sharing.

Can you play word hopscotch?

Focus: vowel digraphs ‘ai/ay’ and ‘oi/oy’, as in *rain/play, oil/boy*

You will need:

Access online resources at My Rising Stars: www.risingstars-uk.com

- Printout of Reminder bubbles
- Cut-out cards resource for groups of children
- Whiteboards and pens
- Chalk and beanbags
- Odd one out train resource per child

In a nutshell

Teacher subject knowledge for this unit:

The digraphs ‘ai’ and ‘oi’ are virtually never used at the end of English words (‘ay’ and ‘oy’ are used for those sounds at the end of words and at the end of syllables).

Word list

ai	ay		oi	oy
rain	day	lay	oil	boy
wait	play	may	join	toy
train	say	pay	coin	enjoy
paid	way	hay	point	annoy
afraid	stay		soil	joy
			foil	

1 Introduce/Review

- Explain to the children that they are learning to spell two different sounds this week.
- Tell them the first sound is in the words *play* and *wait*. Ask the class if they can help you sound out these two words to find the common digraph sound.
- Once the class has found the ‘ai/ay’ sound, ask them in pairs to sound out and find the ‘ai/ay’ sound in words you say. Do this for the words *stay, train, pay* and *afraid.*
- Tell the class that the other sound they are looking at this week is in the words *oil* and *boy*. Ask the class if they can help find the common sound in these two words.
- Once the class has found the ‘oi/oy’ sound, ask them in pairs to sound out and find the ‘oi/oy’ sound in words you say. Do this for the words *join, toy, coin* and *enjoy*.

2 Teach

- Write on the whiteboard *hay* and *wait* and, using sound buttons, ask the class to help you sound them out.
- Explain to the class that the digraph ‘ai/ay’ is spelled differently in each word, even though it sounds the same.
- Write on the whiteboard *play* and underline the digraph ‘ay’. Ask the children where in the word is the ‘ai/ay’ sound in *play* and *hay*. Explain that when the ‘ai/ay’ sound is at the end of a word it is usually spelled ‘ay’. Demonstrate this by asking the children to help sound out and spell the words *say, way* and *may.*
- Write on the whiteboard ‘paid’ and again highlight the digraph ‘ai’. Ask the children if the ‘ai/ay’ sound is still at the end of the word and explain that when the ‘ai/ay’ sound is in the middle of the word it is usually spelled ‘ai’. Ask the children to help sound out and spell *rain* and *train.*
- Explain to the class that the rules are usually the same for the sound ‘oi/oy’.
- Say the word *toy* and ask the class where the ‘oi/oy’ sound is found in the word. Ask them to discuss and feed back which spelling they should use when the ‘oi/oy’ sound is at the end of the word. Repeat with *joy* and *annoy.*
- Say the word *coin* and discuss that since the ‘oi/oy’ sound is in the middle of the word it needs to be spelled ‘oi’.
- Ask the class to help you spell *soil, foil* and *point*. Reinforce how the children knew which grapheme to use.

Challenge!

Use the Spelling Fox Challenge: Can you play word hopscotch? to kick off or consolidate the learning. The children must help the Spelling Fox find the correct answers! Access online via My Rising Stars.

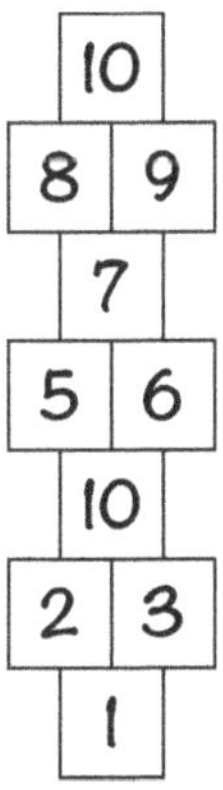

- Show the class and display the Reminder bubbles resource (see You will need) as a prompt for their work.

3 Practise

- Give groups of children a set of cut-out word cards from the Card resource (see You will need) and ask them to muddle them up and turn them upside down in the middle of the group.
- Explain to the class that the children should take it in turns to choose one card to read to the rest of the group. Explain that they should sound it out carefully, blend the sounds and say the word.
- Remind the class to use the Reminder bubbles resource to help them spell the sound correctly on their whiteboards.
- When the group has written the word, the child with the card needs to check the spellings. Any errors should be corrected.
- This continues until the group has spelled all the words correctly.

4 Apply

Activity 1: Word hopscotch

- Take the children outside, if weather permits, or to the sports hall.
- If outside, use chalk to draw four hopscotch grids with no numbers. Paper could be used for the sports hall floor.
- Divide the children into four groups and give each group a different digraph ('ai', 'ay', 'oi', 'oy'). Ask the groups to write one word that uses their sound on to each square of their hopscotch grid. A word list may need to be provided or children may need some suggestions.
- Show the children how to play hopscotch, hopping on the single squares and jumping on the double squares. Say the word on the first square and then throw a beanbag onto this square. Jump over where the beanbag lands onto squares 2 and 3, then hop and jump to the top of the grid, turn around and hop and jump back, again jumping over where the beanbag has landed.
- Take turns to play, throwing the beanbag onto the next square each time.
- Children swap hopscotch grids to play with a different group of words.

Activity 2: Find my family

- Give each child a word card from the Card resource and ask them to stand in a space around the classroom.
- Ask them to sound out their word and decide if they have the 'ai/ay' or the 'oi/oy' sound.
- Ask them to find all the words that use the same sound as their word as quickly as possible and sit down together.
- Once the children are all in groups, ask them to now divide themselves into the different spelling of their sound, i.e. 'oi'/'oy' and 'ai'/'ay'.
- Ask the children to check their groups for any words not using their sound and spelling.
- Repeat activity, giving the children different words.

5 Review

Activity 3: Odd one out train

- Give each child the Odd one out train resource (see You will need) and ask them to sound out the words, blend the sounds to say the word and then find the odd one out in each group. Remind them that they are looking for words using the 'ai/ay' sound or words using the 'oi/oy' sound.
- Demonstrate the first example on the whiteboard. Explain to the children that they need to colour the words that have the same sound and that the odd one out should be left uncoloured.
- Review the work as a class, highlighting the uncoloured carriages.

Can you reveal the picture?

Focus: vowel digraphs 'ee/oo'; and 'ea' (long), 'ea' (short)

You will need:

Access online resources at My Rising Stars: www.risingstars-uk.com

- Picture cards resource cut out
- Word list cards for groups
- 'ee/oo' reveal resource for each child
- 'ea/ea' reveal resource for each child
- Green, brown and yellow pencils

In a nutshell

Teacher subject knowledge for this unit:

Very few words end with the letters 'oo', although the few that do are often words that primary children in year 1 will encounter, e.g. *zoo*.

Word list

ee	oo	ea	ea
see	food	sea	head
tree	pool	dream	bread
green	moon	meat	meant
meet	zoo	each	instead
week	soon	read (present)	read (past tense)
	spoon	eat	feather

1 Introduce/Review

- Tell the class that this week they are learning three different sounds and that their task is to find the sounds from the pictures.
- Give the pictures from Picture card resource (see You will need) out to different children in the class. Ask these children to talk to a partner or small group about what word this picture might show.
- Ask the child with the tree picture to come and stick it on the whiteboard. Ask them what they think it shows and sound out the word 't-r-ee' with the class.
- Highlight the 'ee' digraph and ask if anyone else has a picture that might use the 'ee' sound. Support the class to find *green, meet, sea, meat* and *dream*. Place these pictures all together and highlight in each the 'ee/ea' sound.
- Repeat this activity for the 'oo' digraphs *moon, pool* and *food*.
- Repeat this activity for the 'ea' digraphs *bread, feather* and *head*.

2 Teach

- Show the grouped picture cards from the previous session.
- Ask the children to help you write 'm-oo-n' on the whiteboard. Highlight the 'oo' digraph. Repeat for *spoon* and *zoo*.
- Write the word *head* on the whiteboard and underline the digraph 'ea'. Ask the children to help you write *bread* and *meant* on the whiteboard.
- Show the group of pictures using the 'ee/ea' sounds. Explain that there are different ways of making the 'ee/ea' sound and it can be spelled 'ee' or 'ea'. Demonstrate this with *see* and *sea*, explaining the meaning of each.
- Highlight the different pronunciations but same spelling of the 'ea' digraph in *bread* and *meat*.
- Look at each picture and ask the children to help you sort them into 'ee' and 'ea' spellings. Take ideas from the class as to which spelling is correct for each word and write each word on the whiteboard under 'ee' or 'ea' headings to reinforce.

Challenge!

Use the Spelling Fox Challenge: Can you reveal the picture? to kick off or consolidate the learning. The children must help the Spelling Fox find the correct answers! Access online via My Rising Stars.

- Write the word *read* on the whiteboard and ask the children to sound it out and say the word to a partner. Take feedback as to what the class thinks it says. Explain that it can be said with a long or a short 'ea' sound and can be used to mean read (long 'ea' sound – present tense) or read (short 'ea' sound – past tense).

3 Practise

- Give groups of children one list of words all containing one of the sounds from the Word list card resource (see You will need).
- Tell the children to check they all know the sound that they have been given.
- Within their groups, the children take it in turns to 'be the teacher' and choose one of their words. This child sounds out the word for the rest of the group to write on their whiteboards or in their spelling journals. The 'teacher' child should then show the word, and the rest of the group should check their spelling and correct it if necessary.
- Swap lists of words between groups so all children have a chance to write at least two words using each sound.

4 Apply

Activity 1: Reveal the secret – ee/oo?

- Tell the children that you have a challenge for them. Show them the 'ee/oo' reveal resource (see You will need) and tell them that there is a hidden picture in the outline they need to reveal.
- Tell the children that they need to colour any word that uses the 'ee' sound green and any word that uses the 'oo' sound blue to uncover the picture.
- Children should reveal a tree picture using their green colour.

Activity 2: Reveal the secret – ea/ea?

- Remind children of the word they did in Activity 1.
- Explain that today they are working with the 'ea/ea' sound. Show them the 'ea/ea' reveal resource (see You will need) and remind them that there is a hidden picture in the outline that they need to reveal.
- Tell the children that they need to colour any word that uses the short 'ea' sound brown and any word that uses the long 'ea' sound yellow to uncover the picture.
- Children should reveal a head picture using their brown colour.

5 Review

- Dictate the following sentences for the children to write on their whiteboards or in their spelling journals:

  She enjoys the bread.
  I eat my food with a spoon.
  The tree is green.
  They swim in the pool.

Can you make words from flowers?

Focus: vowel trigraphs ‘air’, ‘igh’, ‘ear’, as in *hair, high, dear*

You will need:

Access online resources at My Rising Stars: www.risingstars-uk.com

- Flower pair resource per pair or for whiteboard display
- Whiteboards and pens

In a nutshell

Teacher subject knowledge for this unit:

The sounds taught this week each comprise three letters and are referred to as ‘trigraphs’.

Word list

air	igh	ear
air	high	dear
fair	night	hear
pair	light	beard
hair	bright	near
chair	right	year
lair	fight	fear

1 Introduce/Review

- Tell the children that this week they are learning some ‘trigraphs’.
- Explain that trigraphs are three letters put together to make one sound.
- Tell the class that the first trigraph is ‘air’ and write it on the whiteboard. Ask the class if they can think of any words that use the ‘air’ sound. Give them time to discuss this and make a list of any words on the whiteboard that have this sound and use the spelling ‘air’. Keep words that use a different spelling of the sound separate.
- Repeat this with ‘ear’.
- Repeat this with ‘igh’. Children could be guided to add the ‘t’ on to the end of the ‘igh’ trigraph to help find more words, e.g. *light, night.*
- Display the list of words on the working wall.

2 Teach

- Write the trigraph ‘air’ on the whiteboard. Sound each letter out individually and explain that they do not need to do this because when we see these three letters we need to remember they make the ‘air’ sound.
- Ask the children to practise writing and saying the ‘air’ sound. Add ‘f’, ‘p’ and ‘h’ on to the front and practise sounding out these words using the ‘air’ sound. In pairs, practise writing these three words – *fair, pair* and *hair* – on individual whiteboards.
- Repeat this for the ‘igh’ and ‘ear’ sounds.

3 Practise

- Write the three trigraph spellings on the whiteboard ‘air’, ‘igh’ and ‘ear’.
- Tell the children that you are going to say a word and they need to decide which trigraph spelling the word contains.
- Say the word *chair* and ask the children which trigraph it contains. Ask them to write just the trigraph on their whiteboards and then to show you. Explain that they do not have to write the full word, just listen to the sound it uses and write just that on their whiteboards.
- Repeat with words from the word list and using the three different trigraphs.

Challenge!

Use the Spelling Fox Challenge: Can you make words from flowers? to kick off or consolidate the learning. The children must help the Spelling Fox find the correct answers! Access online via My Rising Stars.

4 Apply

Activity 1: Flower pair

- Show the children Flower pair resource (see You will need). Explain that the three flowers on the sheet can help the children make different words using this week's trigraphs.
- Demonstrate using the first flower to use a letter from one petal together with the trigraph to make a word. Demonstrate using the word *lair* and explain the meaning of this word.
- Ask the children to make as many words as they can from each flower and write these in their spelling journals.

Activity 2: Make me a sentence

- Ask the children to use all their words from Activity 1 to orally compose a sentence.
- Demonstrate choosing one word and making a sentence using this word, e.g. *I like the fun fair.*
- Challenge the children to make a sentence using a word from each trigraph group, e.g. *In the night I can hear the foxes in their lair.*
- The children could record their sentences using a digital tablet and some of these could be shared with the class at the end of the session.

5 Review

Activity 3: Trigraph bingo

- Ask the children to divide their whiteboards into six squares.
- Tell the children to choose six different words from Activity 1 and write one in each square. Encourage the children to use at least one word from each trigraph group.
- Tell the children that when they hear their word they can cross it out and they should say 'bingo' when they have crossed out all their words.
- Start by saying, *"This word has the 'igh' sound and has an 'h' at the start so this word is …?"* At this point, ask the children to volunteer the word *high*. Repeat this for all the words.
- Continue until one child has completed their bingo board.

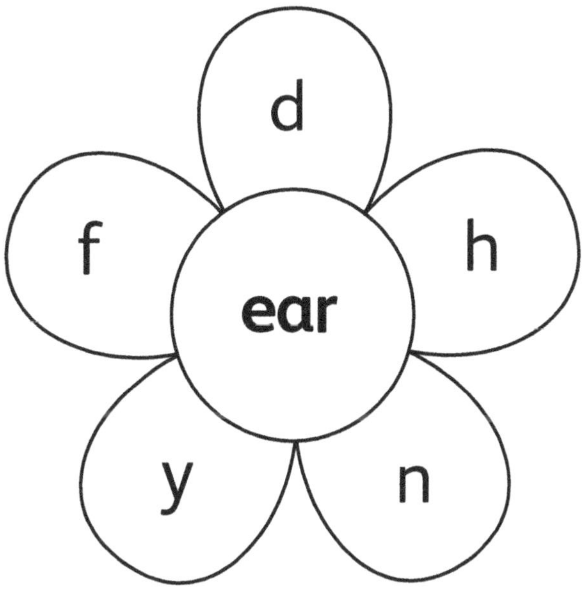

Can you help Drew in his rescue?

Focus: vowel digraph ‘ew’ and ‘ue’, as in *new, blue*

You will need:

Access online resources at My Rising Stars: www.risingstars-uk.com

- Off to the rescue! story for display
- Spelling roll playing board for each child
- Roll race playing board, one per three children
- Dice
- Whiteboards and pens
- Fill with ‘ew/ue’ resource per child
- Coloured pencils

In a nutshell

Teacher subject knowledge for this unit:

Both the /u:/ and /ju:/ (‘oo’ and ‘yoo’) sounds can be spelled as ‘ue’ and ‘ew’. If words end in the ‘oo’ sound, ‘ue’ and ‘ew’ are more common spellings than ‘oo’.

Word list

ew		ue	
new	threw	blue	Tuesday
few	blew	clue	argue
grew	chew	true	glue
flew	stew	rescue	
drew			

1 Introduce/Review

- Tell the children that you have a short story to read to them and they need to listen to see if they can hear any repeated sounds.
- Read the story ‘Off to the rescue!’ (see You will need).
- Ask the class if they spotted any repeated sounds and support them in finding the ‘ew/ue’ sound.
- Repeat the story and ask the children to put their thumbs up when they hear the ‘ew/ue’ sound.
- Show the passage on the whiteboard and, as you read, ask children to come and highlight the words with the ‘ew/ue’ sounds. Also highlight that the words *to* and *do* use the same sound but are spelled differently.
- Display the highlighted passage on the working wall.

2 Teach

- Write the words *new* and *clue* on the whiteboard, underlining the digraphs ‘ew’ and ‘ue’.
- Explain that both these words use the ‘oo’ sound but are spelled in different ways. Explain that when words end in this ‘oo’ sound they are generally spelled with an ‘ew’ or a ‘ue’.
- Go through the highlighted passage from the previous session and sort the words into whether they use the digraph ‘ew’ or ‘ue’.
- Look at the word *Tuesday* and explain that this has the ‘oo’ sound in the middle of the word. Ask the children to practise writing this word on their whiteboards.

3 Practise

- Give each child a copy of the Spelling roll playing board resource (see You will need). Tell the children that they need to write one word in each box. All the words that they write should contain the ‘oo’ sound spelled ‘ew’ or ‘ue’. They should try to use all the words in the word list and each column should contain different words.
- Explain that, by writing the words, it will help them practise the spellings and that they will use their completed sheets next lesson.
- Display the word list to support the children in this activity.

Challenge!

Use the Spelling Fox Challenge: Can you help Drew in his rescue? to kick off or consolidate the learning. The children must help the Spelling Fox find the correct answers! Access online via My Rising Stars.

4 Apply

Activity 1: Spelling roll

- Give the children their copy of the Spelling roll playing board from the previous session.
- Tell the children that they are going to play 'Spelling roll' using their playing boards.
- Demonstrate how to play the game with a child. Roll the dice and show that if it lands on number four your partner reads out (from your own playing board) the first word in the fourth column for you to write on the whiteboard. Ask your partner to check your spelling using your playing board. If it is correct you can colour in that word on your playing board. (Alternatively, children could place a counter over the word they have spelled correctly.)
- Your partner then rolls the dice and you take their playing board ready to read out the relevant word. Remind children to each use a different colour.
- The first person to complete one column on their playing board wins the game.
- Remind the children that with the words *blue/blew* they need to tell their partner whether they should write the colour or whether they should write the action of the wind.

Activity 2: Roll race!

- Explain that this game is played very much like Activity 1, but in this game it is a race to spell the words correctly.
- This may need demonstrating at the front of the class before the activity begins.
- Give groups of three children the Roll race playing board (see You will need).
- One child rolls the dice and reads the first uncoloured word in that column number.
- The other two children now race to write the word on their whiteboards correctly first.
- The first child checks the spelling and the child who answered fastest, with the correct spelling, colours in that word on the playing board. The children swap roles and continue, each colouring words that they have won in different colours.
- If the dice is rolled and the column is completely filled, the child can choose to ask any uncoloured word on the board.
- Continue until the board is completely coloured and the child with the most coloured squares wins the game.

5 Review

- Show the children the two pictures on the Fill with 'ew/ue' resource (see You will need).
- Explain that they need to write words that use the 'ew' spelling in the picture of the wind, and words that use the 'ue' spelling in the picture of the question mark.
- Encourage the children to make their writing fancy and to use colours to make it interesting.
- When finished, ask the children to swap pictures to review each other's work. Ask the class if they can find the word *drew* and *Tuesday* in their partner's pictures. Repeat with other words, encouraging the children to check the spelling of the words and to tell their partner if they find a spelling error.

Can you write in rainbow colours?

Focus: revision of digraphs from units 4–8, Autumn term

You will need:

Access online resources at My Rising Stars: www.risingstars-uk.com

- Revision word cards cut out
- Bag
- Help the horse playing board per pair
- Dice and counters
- Whiteboard and pens

In a nutshell

Teacher subject knowledge for this unit:

Revision of digraphs learned in units 4–8.

1 Introduce/Review

- Tell the children that this week they are going to use some of the sounds that they learned last term: 'ff', 'll', 'ss', 'zz', 'ck', 'ar', 'or', 'ow', 'ou', 'oa', 'ow', 'er', 'ur'.
- Cut out the word cards from the Revision word card resource and place them in a bag (see You will need).
- Pass the bag around the circle and chant the rhyme:

  We are learning how to spell.
  We can do it very well.
  We are looking for a sound.
  Is this the word in which it's found?
- At the end of the rhyme, the child holding the bag picks a card and reads the word. The whole class checks the word and then together sounds it out using the digraph in the word.
- Remind the children of the digraph in this word and ask if they can remember any other word using the same digraph. Help them recall at least two other words in this digraph family. Write these under the digraph heading on the whiteboard.
- Repeat with all the remaining words.

2 Teach

- Remind the children of all the digraphs that they found and remembered in the previous session.
- Recap each of the digraphs, checking the children know how to pronounce them and say them correctly.
- For each digraph, give an example and ask the children to help you sound it out and write it on the whiteboard.

3 Practise

- Ask the children to write a range of words using the different digraphs in different funny styles. Words should include: *smell, puff, jazz, horn, scar, growl, around, soap, throw, person, winter, turn.*
- The children should be asked to write the words in one of the following funny styles:

  Write with your other hand.
  Rainbow-write the word (this involves first writing the word in one colour then, using a different colour, copy close to the original coloured letters, and then repeat again with another different colour).
  Write the word with your eyes closed.
  Write the word in a fancy way.
  Write the word in capital letters.
  Write each letter in a different colour.

Challenge!

Use the Spelling Fox Challenge: Can you write in rainbow colours? to kick off or consolidate the learning. The children must help the Spelling Fox find the correct answers! Access online via My Rising Stars.

4 Apply

Activity 1: Help the horse reach the park

- Give pairs of children the Help the horse playing board (see You will need) and a dice.
- Demonstrate rolling the dice and moving a counter the correct number of squares from the start of the board.
- Tell the children that they then need to say the word correctly, cover it over and then write it correctly. Demonstrate this and ask a child to check your spelling.
- Explain to the children that if they get the word correct they can stay where they are, but if they get it wrong they must move back to the square they started their turn on.
- Pairs of children play the game, continuing until one player reaches the park.
- This activity can be repeated with children landing on different squares.

Activity 2: Sentence maker

- Give out the playing boards from Activity 1, together with a dice.
- This time ask the children to play in pairs with another pair.
- The game is played very much like Activity 2, but when a pair of children roll the dice and land on a square, they need to orally compose a sentence using the word in the square on which they have landed. Demonstrate this with a pair of children.
- The other pair of children needs to check that the sentence makes sense. If the sentence does make sense then the pair can leave their counter on the new square. If it does not then they need to return their counter to the original position.
- This game can then be played with children writing their sentences in their spelling journals.

5 Review

- Dictate the following sentences for the children to write in their spelling journals:

  Today I will pack a brown coat for Mum.
  She said they hurt her.
  In the summer we do not get snow.
  He went out into the garden and fell.

Can you colour the petals?

Focus: revision of digraphs and trigraphs

You will need:

Access online resources at My Rising Stars: www.risingstars-uk.com

- Revision word cards cut out
- Bag
- Spell 'n' roll prompt for display on whiteboard
- Choose a word resource for display on whiteboard
- Colour my petals resource for each child

In a nutshell

Teacher subject knowledge for this unit:

Revision of sounds learned in weeks 9–12.

1 Introduce/Review

- Tell the children that this week they are going to use some of the sounds that they learned last term 'ai', 'ay', 'oi', 'oy', 'ee', 'oo', 'ea', 'air', 'igh', 'ear', 'ew', 'ue'.
- Cut out the Revision word cards and place them in a bag (see You will need).
- Pass the bag around the circle and chant the rhyme:

  We are learning how to spell.
  We can do it very well.
  We are looking for a sound.
  Is this the word in which it's found?
- At the end of the rhyme, the child holding the bag picks a card and reads the word. The whole class checks the word and then together sounds it out using the digraph/trigraph in the word.
- Remind the children of the digraph/trigraph in this word and ask if they can remember any other words using the same digraph/trigraph. Help them recall at least two other words in this digraph/trigraph family. Write these under the digraph/trigraph heading on the whiteboard.
- Repeat with all the remaining words.

2 Teach

- Remind the children of all the digraphs/trigraphs that they found and remembered in the previous session.
- Recap each of the digraphs/trigraphs, checking children know how to pronounce them and say them correctly.
- For each digraph/trigraph, give an example and ask the children to help you sound it out and write it on the whiteboard.

3 Practise

- Give the children the cut out Revision word cards in small groups.
- Demonstrate one child choosing a card and reading it out to the rest of the group, who should write it down on their whiteboards or in their spelling journals.
- The first child should then show the word and check the group's spelling. Children should re-write the word correctly if they have made an error.
- Children should take it in turns to choose a card to read out.

Challenge!

Use the Spelling Fox Challenge: Can you colour the petals? to kick off or consolidate the learning. The children must help the Spelling Fox find the correct answers! Access online via My Rising Stars.

4 Apply

Activity 1: Spell 'n' roll

- Remind the children of the funny writing they did in week 1.
- Tell them that today they are going to be doing their own funny writing using the words they are revising this week.
- Display the Spell 'n' roll prompt resource on the whiteboard (see You will need).
- Demonstrate rolling a dice and selecting the relevant style of writing which relates to the number on the dice.
- Now tell the class a word which you would like written in this style and demonstrate doing this.
- Give each pair of children a dice so they could be writing the same word in a different style.
- You can either give the class the words verbally, or the words could be written in a list on the whiteboard. In this case the children would need to be encouraged to look once at the word, write it in the relevant style without looking again and then to check their spelling.

Activity 2: Complete the sentence

- Show the children the Choose a word resource (see You will need).
- Ask the children in pairs to read the words in the box at the top of the sheet. Check for correct pronunciation.
- Ask the children to copy the sentences into their spelling journals, filling the gap with one of the words from the box. Remind the children that the sentence must make sense and that each word can only be used once.

5 Review

Activity 3: Colour my petals

- Show the children the Colour my petals resource (see You will need).
- Explain that for each flower they should look at the word in each petal and check whether it uses the same digraph/trigraph in the centre. If it makes a word and it is spelled correctly, they should colour in that petal.
- Demonstrate completing the first flower and showing which words are correct and should be coloured, or which are incorrectly spelled / do not use the digraph/trigraph and should be left blank.
- Ask,the children to complete the remaining flowers independently.

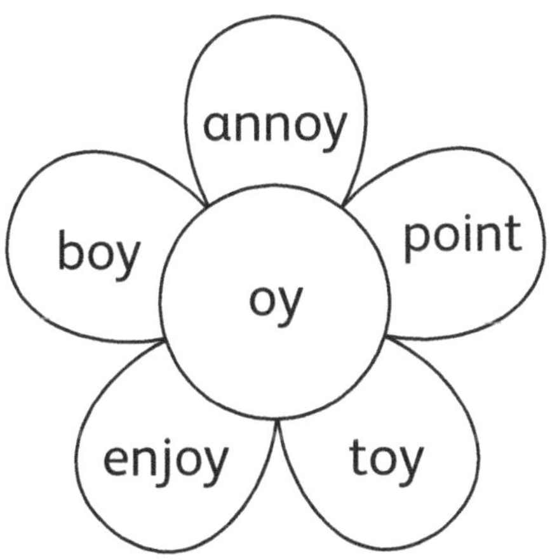

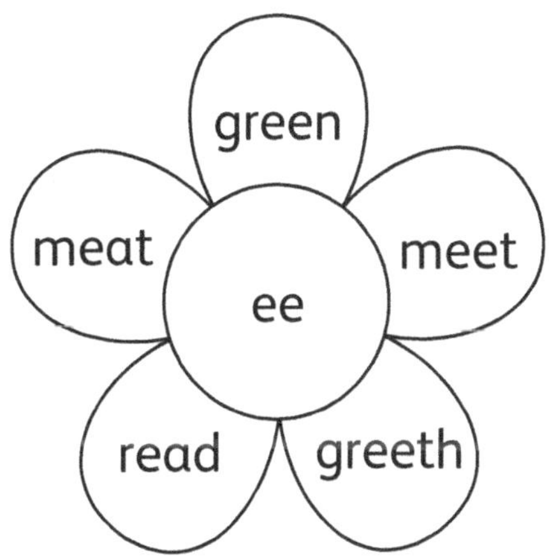

Can you find a tricky one?

Focus: common exception words

You will need:

Access online resources at My Rising Stars: www.risingstars-uk.com

- Bubble secret resource per child
- Exception cards resource cut out per group
- Beanbags
- Magnetic letters or mini sticky notes
- Whiteboards and pens

In a nutshell

Teacher subject knowledge for this unit:

This week focuses on words which are not phonetically decodable. Generally the grapheme-phoneme correspondences do not fit in with what has been taught so far. Children need to be taught to learn these words in different ways and to become familiar with them by sight.

Word list

are	so	has	clue
were	was	by	true
his	is	my	here
no	stew	you	there
go	our	your	where

1 Introduce/Review

- Explain to the children that this week they will be looking at trickier words and remind them of some of the words used in unit 3, Autumn term. These words could be displayed.
- Give the children a copy of Bubble secret resource (see You will need).
- Tell the children that there is a hidden letter ('X' for exception) which will be revealed when they connect the bubbles.
- Ask the children to colour all the words that are spelled correctly in one colour and all the incorrect words in another colour.
- Challenge them to find the hidden letter.

2 Teach

- Write *are, no, was, by, you* and *here* on the whiteboard.
- Go through each word, try to sound them out and remind the children that these are difficult words to sound out and are called 'exception words'.
- Ask the children to try to learn each of these words with a partner and give them time to do this. Discuss as a class the strategies that they have used to learn these words, e.g. remembering it visually, phonetically or using a rhyme to help.
- Explain that each of these words is part of a 'family group' with other words which sound and are spelled very similarly.
- Show *no, go* and *so* and ask the children to explain why these words are similar.
- Explain that knowing how to spell *no* helps us to spell *go*.
- Show the other family groups by writing them on the whiteboard. Ask the children to look at the groups and decide how they can learn the spellings. Give them time to discuss and practise these spellings.

3 Practise

- Ask the children to choose a word from the class whiteboard and write it on their own whiteboard.
- Children should then stand in a circle and place their whiteboards on the floor in the middle so that all the words are visible.
- Give one child a beanbag.

Challenge!
Use the Spelling Fox Challenge: Can you find a tricky one? to kick off or consolidate the learning. The children must help the Spelling Fox find the correct answers! Access online via My Rising Stars.

- The child with the beanbag throws the beanbag to land on one of the whiteboards. The child should then remove the beanbag and hold the whiteboard so that the word is visible.
- The child needs to then say the word which should be repeated by the class.
- This whiteboard can then be removed.
- This child then throws the beanbag to another child who does the same.
- Repeat until there are no whiteboards left.

4 Apply

Activity 1: Oral Sentences

- Give small groups of children a set of Exception cards cut out (see You will need).
- Place the cards face up in front of the group.
- Ask the group to orally compose a sentence that uses at least two of the exception word cards, e.g. *there is a pig in your garden.*
- Once they have composed their sentence they can remove the words used.
- Continue until they have composed sentences using all of the words.

Activity 2: Magnetic words

- Give small groups of children a set of magnetic letters, or mini sticky notes, and a set of Exception cards.
- Ask one child from the group to choose a card and, without showing the group, read it out. The rest of the group together makes this word using the magnetic letters. The first child then checks the word and corrects it if necessary.
- The children swap roles and continue until all the words have been spelled out using the magnetic letters.

5 Review

Activity 3: Have we found a tricky one?

- Tell the children that today they are going on an 'exception hunt'.
- Take the children outdoors to the playground. (This activity could also be run indoors using a sports hall and with words written on paper or whiteboards.)
- Mark out the boundary of the area that you will be using and tell the children where they are allowed to go for this activity.
- Verbally give each child one of the exception words from this week's word list. Some children may need extra support and to be given a word card.
- Ask the children to go and write the word they have been given on the playground in the allowed area, using a piece of chalk, and then to draw a circle around it. Demonstrate this by writing *here* and then drawing a circle around it.
- Go around the words and check for accurate spelling. Correct any if necessary.
- As a class all say the following chant:

  We are going on a word hunt.
  Can we find an exception word?
  Let's stop and look around.
  Have we found a tricky one?

- At this point demonstrate by throwing a beanbag onto one of the circled exception words, e.g. *your.*
- Then demonstrate sounding the word out, showing that it does not fit the normal rules and then saying the word.
- Put the children into small groups, each with a beanbag, to continue this activity in the same way. Several groups could use the same area or, alternatively, two separate areas could be used and the groups could repeat the activity in both areas.

Can you do word addition?

Focus: vowel digraph 'oo' and compound words

You will need:

Access online resources at My Rising Stars: www.risingstars-uk.com

- 'oo' sort resource and word cards per child
- Compound addition resource per child
- Sticky notes and whiteboards

In a nutshell

Teacher subject knowledge for this unit:

Compound words are two words joined together. Each part of the longer word is spelled as it would be if it were on its own.

Word list

oo		compound words	
book	good	football	blackberry
took	cook	playground	sunset
foot	look	farmyard	
wood	wool	bedroom	

1 Introduce/Review

- Explain to the children that words can be divided into 'beats'. These 'beats' are called syllables. Explain that some words have just one syllable and some words have more than one syllable.
- Demonstrate clapping the syllables in *well* and *pocket*.
- Ask the class to help you clap the syllables in *rabbit*, *carrot* and *thunder*.
- Now choose a child and clap the syllables in their name.
- Ask the children to take turns in clapping the syllables in a partner's name.
- Ask the children to go around the classroom and clap the syllables in different people's names.
- Introduce *foot* and *ball* and ask the children to explain what happens with the word *football*. Explain that two simple words put together without a space are called 'compound words' and they then become words with more than one syllable.
- Repeat clapping syllables for *play*, *ground* and *playground*; *farm*, *yard* and *farmyard*; *bed*, *room* and *bedroom*.

2 Teach

- Write the digraph 'oo' on the whiteboard and ask the children to help you say it. Explain that there are two different ways of sounding out: 'oo', as in *food*, and 'oo', as in *foot*.
- Tell the children that today they are learning the 'oo' sound, as in *foot*. Ask the children to help you sound out and write *book*, *took* and *foot* on the whiteboard.
- Write on the whiteboard the rest of the 'oo' words from the word list – *wood*, *good*, *cook*, *look*, *wool*. Ask the children to say the words with a partner and listen for correct sounding out, use of the 'oo' sound and correct blending to pronounce the word.
- Now tell the children that you are going to use this sound to make a compound word. Ask the children to help you write *bookshop* and *football* on the whiteboard.

3 Practise

- Give pairs of children a whiteboard with individual letters written on mini sticky notes.
- Ask them to use the letters to make the word that you dictate from the word list.
- Pairs should work together to make the words with their letters.
- Check the boards after every word for accurate spelling.

Challenge!

Use the Spelling Fox Challenge: Can you do word addition? to kick off or consolidate the learning. The children must help the Spelling Fox find the correct answers! Access online via My Rising Stars.

4 Apply

Activity 1: 'oo' sort

- Challenge the children to sort words that use the two different sounds of the 'oo' digraph.
- Give children a copy of the 'oo' sort resource (see You will need) and explain that they need to cut out the word cards and stick them into the correct section corresponding to whether the word uses 'oo' as in *book*, or 'oo' as in *moon*. (Alternatively, the children could sort the word cards onto the correct picture or onto a whiteboard with headings.)
- Go through the words that the children have in each column as a check.

Activity 2: Compound addition

- Remind the children of the 'oo' sounds that they are learning to use in their spelling this week.
- Remind them that many individual words can be put together to make a compound word, e.g. *look* and *out* make *lookout*.
- Tell the class that their challenge today is to create some compound words using words that use the 'oo' sound.
- Show them Compound addition resource (see You will need) and make sure that they know what the pictures represent (*book*, *foot*, *wood*).
- Ask them to complete the sheet, creating compound words on the sheet or in their spelling journals.

5 Review

- Dictate the following sentences to the class for them to write in their spelling journal:

  He was a good cook.
  I read my book in my bedroom.
  There was a man in the farmyard.
  Today I left footprints in the sand at sunset.

Can you find the ‘au’ and ‘aw’?

Focus: vowel digraph ‘au’ and ‘aw’, as in *author, saw*

You will need:

Access online resources at My Rising Stars: www.risingstars-uk.com

- ‘au/aw’ picture cards per group
- Four-in-a-row ‘au/aw’ playing board per pair
- Counters
- Whiteboards and pens

In a nutshell

Teacher subject knowledge for this unit:

When the ‘aw’ precedes an ‘n’ or ‘l’ it is usually spelled ‘aw’.

Word list

au		aw	
author	auction	saw	claw
August	caution	yawn	straw
astronaut	audio	crawl	lawn
autumn		draw	dawn
		raw	prawn

1 Introduce/Review

- Give groups of children the six pictures from ‘au/aw’ picture cards resource (see You will need).
- Ask them to decide in their group what word each picture might represent.
- Tell the class that the words from each picture all share a common sound.
- Ask them to see if they can decide what this sound might be.
- When the class have had time to discuss these pictures, take feedback and tell them, if necessary, what each picture shows.
- Highlight the ‘aw/au’ sound.
- Ask the class to come up with any other words that use the ‘aw/au’ sound. Write these on the whiteboard to highlight the use of the ‘aw/au’ sound, keeping words that use the similar sound but different spelling separate.

2 Teach

- Remind the class of the sound that they are using this week.
- Write ‘aw’ and ‘au’ on the whiteboard and explain that each of these uses the same sound.
- Explain that the ‘aw’ spelling is the most common before an ‘l’ or an ‘n’.
- Demonstrate this by sounding out and recording on the whiteboard *yawn, lawn* and *crawl.*
- Show the words *August*, *astronaut* and *autumn* and practise writing these on the whiteboard with the class.
- Remind children that *August* uses a capital letter because it is a month.

3 Practise

Activity 1: Find the ‘au’ and ‘aw’

- Show the children the Four-in-a-row ‘au/aw’ playing board from the resources (see You will need).
- Explain that on the board all the words have the ‘aw/au’ sound in them, but that some of them use ‘aw’ and some use ‘au’.
- Ask children to work in pairs. One child should sound out the word and say it to their partner. Their partner should decide if it uses the ‘aw’ or ‘au’ spelling. They should then check whether they are correct. Demonstrate this activity first.

Challenge!
Use the Spelling Fox Challenge: Can you find the 'au' and 'aw'? to kick off or consolidate the learning. The children must help the Spelling Fox find the correct answers! Access online via My Rising Stars.

- Ask them to colour the 'aw' words one colour and the 'au' words another colour.
- After the children have completed the task, ask the class if they have found a hidden letter and highlight that the 'aw' sound words should make a 'w' shape in the grid.
- Keep the playing boards for use in Activities 2 and 3.

4 Apply

Activity 2: Four-in-a-row

- Give the children the Four-in-a-row 'au/aw' playing board from the previous session.
- Remind the children that the coloured squares will help them remember which 'aw/au' sound is used in each word.
- Explain that the idea of the game is to connect four words in a row, either horizontally, vertically or diagonally.
- Play the game with a child at the front of the class. Demonstrate choosing a word and saying it correctly to claim the word.
- Children have different coloured counters and place these on the words that they have successfully claimed.
- Explain that if they do not get the word right then the other player has a chance to steal the word by saying it correctly.

Activity 3: Four-in-a-row sentences

- This game is played exactly like Activity 2, but in this game the children need to orally compose a sentence using the word they choose.
- The other player should check to make sure that it makes sense and then the first player can claim the word.
- Take turns to play the game and continue until a player has 'four-in-a-row'.
- Swap partners and replay the game.

5 Review

- Give the children the Four-in-a-row 'au/aw' playing board and some counters.
- Demonstrate choosing a word at random, sounding it out using the 'au/aw' digraph and then covering it over with a counter.
- Ask a child to be your partner and to write this word on their whiteboard whilst it is hidden by the counter.
- Now uncover the word and demonstrate checking it together with your partner. If it is correct then the child who has written the word keeps the counter.
- Ask the children to continue this game in pairs and at the end of the lesson reward the children with the most counters.

Can you make some silly sentences?

Focus: vowel digraph 'ir' and 'oe', as in *girl, toe*

You will need:

Access online resources at My Rising Stars: www.risingstars-uk.com

- 'ir/oe' picture cards cut out per group
- Bag
- 'ir/oe' word cards cut out per group

In a nutshell

Teacher subject knowledge for this unit:

Vowel digraphs 'ir' and 'oe'.

Word list

ir		oe	
girl	fir	toe	hoe
bird	sir	goes	
shirt	dirt		
first	skirt		
third			

1 Introduce/Review

- Tell the children that they are practising using two more sounds in their spelling this week and that their task is to find some words that use these sounds.
- Ask the class to sit in a circle. Place the cut-out 'ir/oe' picture cards (see You will need) into a bag. Explain to the children that all the pictures in the bag represent a word that uses one of these sounds.
- Explain that the bag will be passed around the circle whilst this rhyme is chanted:

  We are learning how to spell.
  We can do it very well.
  We are looking for a sound.
  Is this the word in which it's found?

- When the rhyme finishes, the child holding the bag takes one of the pictures out of the bag.
- This child, together with help from the two children either side, needs to try to decide what word it might be. If they do not get it right then the rest of the class and teacher help to find the word.
- Explain to the class that the two sounds they are learning are 'ir' and 'oe'.
- Divide the pictures into the two groups depending on the sound.

2 Teach

- Write 'ir' on the whiteboard and ask the children to practise saying it and writing it.
- Take the picture of the girl from the previous session and ask the class to help sound out how to write *girl*, and then do the same with *fir* and *sir*.
- Continue with the other 'ir' pictures.
- Now write 'oe' on the whiteboard and tell the children how to pronounce this sound.
- Ask the children to help write *hoe* and *goes* on the whiteboard.
- Explain that whilst *go* uses the 'oe' sound, it does not use this spelling except when we use the word *goes*.
- Keep the words on the whiteboard for display.

3 Practise

- Give groups of children a set of cut-out 'ir/oe' picture cards.
- Ask each group to turn the pictures face down and spread them out on the floor or table.

Challenge!

Use the Spelling Fox Challenge: Can you make some silly sentences? to kick off or consolidate the learning. The children must help the Spelling Fox find the correct answers! Access online via My Rising Stars.

- Demonstrate this activity by choosing a picture, saying what it shows and then as a group writing the word on a whiteboard.
- Children should then use the list of words on the class whiteboard to check their spelling and correct if necessary.
- Ask the children to take it in turns to choose a picture and turn it over, and continue until all the pictures have been used.

4 Apply

Activity 1: Match the word

- Give groups of children the pictures from the 'Practise' session, together with the cut-out 'ir/oe' word cards (see You will need).
- Explain to the class that for each picture card there is a word card that matches and that their task is to find the matching word.
- Explain that for the words *sir*, *goes* and *fir* there are no pictures and that they need to match two identical written words.
- Demonstrate muddling up the cards, turning them face down and spreading them out over the floor or table.
- Explain that for each child's turn they can only flip over two cards and if they match then they get to keep them.
- Explain that if they do not match then the player should turn the cards back over and place them in their original positions. The next player then has a turn.
- Encourage the children to remember where the cards were placed and to find them again when they have a word or picture that matches.
- Continue playing the game until all the pairs have been found.

Activity 2: Hangman

- Make sure the 'ir/oe' word cards are available for the children to see.
- Ask one child to come to the front of the class and to choose a word from the board. Ask this child to draw a dash for each letter in their chosen word. As a class, practise guessing letters that might be in the word.
- Demonstrate how the child should write the letters guessed and how to draw a hangman with each wrong guess.
- Ask the children to complete this activity in pairs.
- Swap and repeat.

5 Review

Activity 3: Silly sentence maker

- Write on the whiteboard the following sentence:

  I saw a… that had a ….
- Ask the children to help you fill in the gaps using some of the words that they have been using today. Ask the children to try to make the sentence funny but still make sense, e.g. *I saw a bird that had a shirt! I saw a girl that had a toe!* (Explain that the children can change a linking word to make the sentence grammatically correct.)
- In pairs give the children a copy of the 'ir/oe' word cards.
- Ask them to use these words to orally compose a silly sentence.
- Then ask them to share their silly sentence with another pair.

Can you link the sounds?

Focus: the /v/ sound and the /η/ sound spelled 'n' before 'k'

You will need:

Access online resources at My Rising Stars: www.risingstars-uk.com

- Word cards cut out
- Sticky notes and whiteboards
- Word search resource per child
- Link-up cards per group
- Dictate me a sentence resource per pair

In a nutshell

Teacher subject knowledge for this unit:

English words rarely end with the letter 'v', so if a word ends with a /v/ sound, the letter 'e' usually needs to be added after the 'v'.
The letter 'n' before a 'k' at the end of a word produces the /η/ sound.

Word list

ending 've'		/η/	
love	serve	bank	sunk
have	nerve	think	link
give	active	honk	
live	captive		

1 Introduce/Review

- Tell the class that this week they are learning two sounds and you have words from each sound to give them.
- Tell them that you have muddled up the words and it is their challenge to put them back into two groups, depending on the sound they use.
- Show them the words *live* and *link* and say that these words contain different sounds. Explain how to pronounce both words and that the final 'e' of *live* is silent.
- Give groups the cut-out Word cards from the resources (see You will need).
- Encourage the children to sound out the words and listen to each other to find the sound that each word uses.
- Look at the groups of words in each sound and stress the /v/ and the /η/ sound in each word.

2 Teach

- Write the word *love* on the whiteboard, sounding every phoneme and underlining the digraph 've'.
- Explain that very few words end in 'v' alone, so the /v/ sound normally has the 've' when at the end of words.
- Ask the class to help you write *have*, *give* and *serve* on the whiteboard whilst they copy on their own whiteboards.
- Show the words *bank* and *think* and explain that the 'n' and 'k' go together to make the /η/ sound.

3 Practise

- Give pairs of children a whiteboard with individual letters written on mini sticky notes.
- Ask them to use the letters to make the word that you dictate from the word list.
- Pairs should work together to make the words with their letters.
- Check the whiteboards after every word for accurate spelling.

Challenge!
Use the Spelling Fox Challenge: Can you link the sounds? to kick off or consolidate the learning. The children must help the Spelling Fox find the correct answers! Access online via My Rising Stars.

4 Apply

Activity 1: Word search

- Show the children the Word search from the resources (see You will need).
- Read through the words and explain any unfamiliar words.
- Explain that each word can only go in one direction: horizontal, vertical or diagonal.
- Demonstrate how to find the first word, how to colour it and cross it off the list at the bottom of the page.

Activity 2: Link-up

- Give groups of children a cut-out set of Link-up cards from the resources (see You will need).
- Tell the class that the words have become separated from their endings and their challenge is to put the words back together so they are spelled correctly and make sense, e.g. 'li' can be joined with 've' or 'nk' to make *live* or *link*.
- Encourage children to sound out the words and say them correctly.
- Look at the words made and check they are correct. Groups could check each other's work.

5 Review

Activity 3: Dictate me a sentence

- Give pairs of children the cut-out sentences from the Dictate me a sentence resource (see You will need).
- Read the sentences as a class, ensuring that the children understand what they are saying and how to pronounce all the words.
- Explain that today the children are going to be the teachers and that they are going to dictate a sentence to their partner to write.
- Demonstrate turning the sentences face down, choosing one and dictating this to a child to write.
- Demonstrate checking the sentence using the original sentence as support.
- Remind the children that not only must they try to spell the words correctly, but that they must always make sure their sentence has a capital letter and a full stop.
- Remind the children that they need to correct their sentences if necessary.

Can you catch the thief?

Focus: vowel digraph 'ie' (/aɪ/) and 'ie' (/iː/), as in *lie, chief*

You will need:

Access online resources at My Rising Stars: www.risingstars-uk.com

- Catch the thief cards cut out, enough for one per child
- Field or pie? resource per child
- Chalk and beanbags
- Write it right cards cut out, per pair or group
- Path through the fields board per child
- Path through the fields (answers) for display

In a nutshell

Teacher subject knowledge for this unit:

Vowel digraph 'ie'.

Word list

ie (/aɪ/)		ie (/iː/)	
lie	cried	chief	thief
pie	tried	field	grief
tie	dried		

1 Introduce/Review

Activity 1: Catch the thief!

- Write up the words from the word list on the whiteboard and sound them out together. Ensure that the children can say all of the words.
- Tell the class that you are going to play 'Catch the thief!'.
- Explain that one person will be given the word 'chief' and they need to go out of the room and wait until they are called in.
- Explain that you will give each child a word (from the Catch the thief cards resource – see You will need) and they need to make sure they can say their word and then hide it behind their back. Some children will have the same word.
- Explain that one child will be given the word *thief*.
- When the chief comes back into the room, they need to ask a child:

  Have you stolen my 'ie' (/aɪ/)?

- The child then needs to say their word after the reply:

  I have the word ...

- The chief has three guesses to find the thief. If they guess correctly then they have another go; if they guess incorrectly then the thief becomes the chief.
- The game continues with the children being given different words.

2 Teach

- Remind the children of the game in Activity 1 and explain that all the words used the digraph 'ie'.
- Write the words *lie* and *pie* on the whiteboard and underline the digraph 'ie'.
- Now write the word *chief* on the whiteboard and underline the digraph 'ie' again. Explain that these two spellings are pronounced differently and ensure that the children can hear and say the different sounds.
- Give the children different words and ask them to tell you which 'ie' sound group it belongs to.
- Sound out and practise writing *field, cried* and *dried.*

3 Practise

- Show the children the Field or pie? resource (see You will need).
- Explain that their challenge is to write the words that use the 'ie' (/aɪ/) sound inside the pie and the words that use the 'ie' (/iː/) sound inside the field.

Challenge!
Use the Spelling Fox Challenge: Can you catch the thief? to kick off or consolidate the learning. The children must help the Spelling Fox find the correct answers! Access online via My Rising Stars.

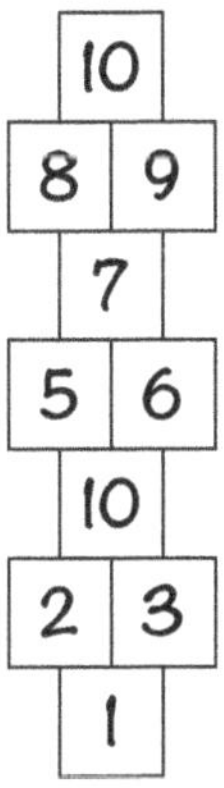

- Encourage the children to use fancy, coloured or bubble writing for the words.
- Check the children have put the correct words inside the pie and the field.

4 Apply

Activity 2: Word hopscotch

- Take the children outside, if weather permits, or to the sports hall.
- Divide the children into groups and use chalk to draw a hopscotch grid for each group. Words could be written on to paper for the sports hall floor.
- Divide the children into groups and give each group an 'ie' group of words but using a different sound. Ask the groups to write one word that uses their sound in each square. A word list may need to be provided or children may need suggestions. Words can be duplicated. Show the children how to play hopscotch. Say the word on the first square and then throw a beanbag on to this square. Jump over where the beanbag lands and hop and jump on to the remaining square to the top of the grid, turn around and hop and jump back.
- Take turns to play, landing on the next square each time.
- Children swap hopscotch grids to play with a different group of words.

Activity 3: Write it right

- Tell the children that today they are going to try to write the words right (correctly) in playing the game 'Write it right'.
- Demonstrate turning the cards from the Write it right resource (see You will need) face down on the floor or table.
- One child chooses a card and reads what it says without showing their partner.
- Their partner now needs to write the word on their whiteboard.
- They show their whiteboard and the first child checks that the word is spelled correctly.
- If it is correct then it can be kept by the child who has written the word. If it is incorrect then it is placed back down with the rest of the cards.
- The game continues until all the cards have been claimed.

5 Review

Activity 4: Path through the fields

- Show the children the Path through the fields resource (see You will need) and explain that they need to colour a pathway through the fields for the chief to get to the pie, using only words from the 'ie' group. Tell them to start on *chief* and end on *pie*.
- Tell them that they cannot step on (or colour) a word that does not include this sound, otherwise the pie will be taken by thief who is waiting at the edge of the fields.
- Demonstrate how to start on the starting stone and to sound out the words on the stones that are next to this stone. Explain that they cannot jump over stones. Demonstrate colouring in the stone with the next correctly spelled word and explain how they then continue until they find the path all the way through the field to reach the end.
- Remind the children that there are other words that include this sound, but they can only colour a word if it is on the path from the chief to the pie.
- Explain that if they get the path correct it will reveal a secret letter.
- Children can compare the path that they have found to reveal the letter 'E'.
- As an alternative this game could be enlarged and played on the floor. Individual 'stones' could be enlarged and cut out and the game played outside or in a sports hall.

Can you solve the crime?

Focus: split digraphs 'a-e', 'e-e', 'i-e', 'o-e', 'u-e'

You will need:

Access online resources at My Rising Stars: www.risingstars-uk.com

- The Crime story for display
- Split digraph and word cards sort per child
- Roll 'n' write cards cut out per group
- Roll 'n' write instructions for display
- Whiteboards and pens

In a nutshell

Teacher subject knowledge for this unit:

These spellings are referred to as split digraphs because the digraph sound is split with a consonant letter between. All these split digraph sounds end with the silent letter 'e'. The initial sound of these digraphs is the capital letter pronunciation of the letter, with the exception of 'u' where both the /u:/ and /ju:/ ('oo' and 'yoo') sounds can be spelled as 'u-e'.

Word list

a-e	e-e	i-e	o-e	u-e
made	these	five	home	June
came	theme	ride	those	rule
same	complete	like	woke	rude
take	compete	time	hope	use
safe	delete	side	hole	tube
	severe	hide	joke	tune
		wide	bone	luke
		fine	stone	flute
		shine	vote	
		crime	stove	
		ripe	stole	
		stripe		
		wise		
		dive		
		fire		

1 Introduce/Review

- Tell the children that this week they are learning about two letters that are called 'split digraphs'. Remind them that neither letter can make the sound alone, so both letters are needed, as they work together.
- Tell the class that there are five letters in the alphabet called vowels and that these are 'a', 'e', 'i', 'o' and 'u'. Tell the class that these are important letters and are used in split digraphs. Explain how each is said when used with split digraphs and give some examples, e.g. *same, five, rude.*
- Tell the class that you have a story to read that uses lots of these words.
- Read the story 'The Crime' from the resources (see You will need), displaying it on the whiteboard.
- Go through the story and highlight any word that uses the long vowel sound, underlining the vowel and the 'e' at the end of the word each time.

2 Teach

- Remind the children of the passage highlighted in the previous session.
- Draw a table with five columns on the whiteboard and ask the children to help you write the five vowels at the top of each column.
- Explain to the children that with split digraphs you need the letter 'e', which is split over another letter. Now write the split digraph headings 'i-e' and 'a-e'.

Challenge!

Use the Spelling Fox Challenge: Can you solve the crime? to kick off or consolidate the learning. The children must help the Spelling Fox find the correct answers! Access online via My Rising Stars.

- Go through the story from the previous lesson and look at each highlighted word. Ask the children to help you sort them into the correct columns.
- A copy of the story could be made, the highlighted words cut out and one given to each child. The children could then come and stick their word into the correct column, depending on the digraph used.
- Alternatively, the children could draw five columns on their own whiteboards and write the words in the correct columns as they are highlighted on the board.

3 Practise

- Give the children the Split digraph sort resource (see You will need).
- Ask the class to cut out the words and stick them into the correct column depending on which digraph is being used. Alternatively, the children could write each word in the relevant column.
- Encourage the children to sound out the words and underline the split digraphs in each word.

4 Apply

Activity 1: Compose me a sentence

- Give groups of children the cut-out Roll 'n' write word cards (see You will need).
- Check that the children can read and understand any unfamiliar vocabulary.
- Ask the children to work in pairs. One child should choose a word and their partner needs to orally compose a sentence that uses this word.
- Demonstrate this and remind the class that the word should make sense in the sentence they create.
- Ask the pairs to feedback to the class with the best sentence that they composed. The class could be challenged to guess which word in the sentence was the one that the child was given to use.

Activity 2: Roll 'n' write

- Give groups of children the cut-out Roll 'n' write word cards.
- Check that the children can read and understand any unfamiliar vocabulary.
- Display the Roll 'n' write instructions sheet (see You will need) and remind the children how they need to write for each dice number.
- One child chooses a word at random from the set of cards. All children have a chance to look at the word and sound it out together as a group.
- The word is then turned face down and a different child rolls the dice.
- The group then writes the word in the style indicated by the dice roll.
- The word is then turned over and the children check their spelling.
- The game continues until all the cards have been used.

5 Review

- Dictate the following sentences for the children to write on whiteboards or in their spelling journals.

  She was made to ride the flume.
  Today I will vote for those I like.
  These jokes are not like mine.
  The dog had a bone and went to hide it.
- After writing each sentence, ask the children to underline the split digraph words.

Can you find the hidden words?

Focus: graphemes 'ph' and 'wh', as in *dolphin, when*

You will need:

Access online resources at My Rising Stars: www.risingstars-uk.com

- 'ph' and 'wh' pictures for display and per child
- 'ph' and 'wh' labels per child
- 'wh' word cards cut out per group
- Hidden word resource per child
- Word art designs for whiteboard display

In a nutshell

Teacher subject knowledge for this unit:

The /f/ sound is not usually spelled as 'ph' in short everyday words, e.g. *fat, fill, fun.*

Word list

ph		wh	
dolphin	phonics	when	wheel
alphabet	graph	where	while
elephant		which	

1 Introduce/Review

- Show the class the 'ph' and 'wh' pictures resource (see You will need) on the whiteboard.
- Focus on the 'ph' pictures and ask the class to tell their partner what each picture shows. Explain the pictures if necessary.
- Ask the class to think about what sound they all have and what sound they might be learning this week.
- Establish with the class the 'ph' sound and sound each word out, stressing the 'ph' sound.
- Now focus them on the two 'wh' pictures and ask what sound these two words have in common.
- Tell the class some more 'wh' words, e.g. *which, where,* and ask them to sound them out in pairs.
- Give them the word *while* and remind them of the split digraph 'i-e' from unit 9. Sound this out as a group.

2 Teach

- Write the word *fun* on the whiteboard. Sound it out and ask the children to identify the 'f' sound. Explain that this is a short everyday word and we normally use the 'f' to spell these kind of words.
- Write the letters 'ph' on the whiteboard and explain that these letters are also pronounced 'f' and are often used for longer words.
- Ask the class to help you write the word *dolphin*, sounding out each phoneme.
- Repeat for the words *elephant* and *graph.*
- Show them the pictures of *wheel* and *when* again and ask them to suggest how to spell these two words.
- Explain that in these words the 'w' sound is spelled 'wh'.
- Demonstrate this spelling in the words *where, which* and *while.*

3 Practise

- Give the children the pictures and labels from both the 'ph' and 'wh' pictures and the 'ph' and 'wh' labels resources (see You will need).
- Ask the children to cut out the pictures and stick the label under the correct picture in their spelling journals.
- Ask the children to then copy the words underneath, underlining the 'ph' and 'wh' sound they are learning this week.

Challenge!
Use the Spelling Fox Challenge: Can you find the hidden words? to kick off or consolidate the learning. The children must help the Spelling Fox find the correct answers! Access online via My Rising Stars.

4 Apply

Activity 1: Pairs

- Give groups of children another set of the cut-out pictures and labels from the 'ph' and 'wh' resources, together with the extra words from the 'wh' word cards resource (see You will need).
- Explain to the class that for each picture there is a label that matches and that their task is to find the match.
- Explain that for the words *where*, *which* and *while* there are no pictures and that they need to match two identical written words.
- Demonstrate muddling up the cards, turning them over face down and spreading them out over the floor or table.
- Explain that on their turn they can only flip over two cards and if they match then they get to keep them.
- Explain that if they do not match then the player should turn them back over and place them in their original positions. The next player then has a turn.
- Encourage the children to remember where the words were placed and to find them again when they have a word that matches.
- Continue playing the game until all the pairs have been found.

Activity 2: Find the hidden word

- Show the children the Hidden word resource (see You will need).
- Explain that each clue leads to a word and that each letter of the word should go in a box in order. Explain that the letters in the vertical column highlighted will then make a new word. They should see if they can find the new word and write it in the space at the bottom of the sheet.
- Remind the children to use the pictures and word list, as well as the clues, to help them.
- If necessary, verbal support can be given with the word choice.
- When the children have found the hidden word (phonics), they should underline the 'ph' sound.

5 Review

- Ask the children to remember some of the words that they have been learning this week.
- Display the list of words on the whiteboard for children to use.
- Show the Word art designs from the resources (see You will need).
- Ask the children to use the words to create a 'funky' design in their spelling journals or on paper for display. Encourage them to use fancy writing, colours and to place words in different directions using different sizes.
- Once the children have completed this for the 'ph' words, encourage them to create something different for the 'wh' words.
- Remind the children that they can write the same word several times for effect.

Can you bag the 'y'?

Focus: words ending in 'y', as in *very, happy, funny*

You will need:

Access online resources at My Rising Stars: www.risingstars-uk.com

- 'y' word cards cut out, per pair
- Bag
- Jumble me up resource per child

In a nutshell

Teacher subject knowledge for this unit:

Words that end in 'y'.

Word list

very	family	body
happy	ugly	windy
funny	oily	dolly
party		

1 Introduce/Review

- Ask the class to sit in a circle. Place the cut-out 'y' word cards (see You will need) into a bag. Explain to the children that all the words in the bag have the same sound and it is the children's challenge to be the first to find the sound that they all use.
- Explain that the bag will be passed around the circle whilst this rhyme is being said:

  We are learning how to spell.
  We can do it very well.
  We are looking for a sound.
  Is this the word in which it's found?

- When the rhyme finishes, the child holding the bag takes one of the pictures out of the bag.
- This child, together with help from the two children either side, needs to sound out the word.
- Highlight that all the words use the 'y' sound at the end of the word.
- Ask the children to think if there are any other words ending in the 'y' sound. These should be written on the whiteboard. Keep those spelled with a 'y' together and display these on the working wall.

2 Teach

- Remind the children of some of the 'y' words they found yesterday and tell them that they are looking at those words that are spelled with a 'y' on the end.
- Ask the children if they can think of any words ending with the 'y' sound. Write these on the whiteboard, keeping any words that are not spelled with a 'y' separate.
- Take individual 'y' words from the word list and ask the children to help you sound them out. Stress the 'y' sound and ask the children to help you by reminding you what letter to use for this sound in each word.

3 Practise

- Read out individual words and ask the children to use their whiteboards or spelling journals to record the words as you dictate them.
- Ask them to underline the 'y' sound.
- Write the words on the whiteboard and ask the children to check their spelling and correct them if necessary.

Challenge!
Use the Spelling Fox Challenge: Can you bag the 'y'? to kick off or consolidate the learning. The children must help the Spelling Fox find the correct answers! Access online via My Rising Stars.

4 Apply

Activity 1: Quick spell

- Ask the class to stand in a circle.
- Explain that this is a quick game and that if the children are not quick they will be out.
- Display the list of 'y' words on the whiteboard.
- Give a soft ball to a child and ask them to choose a word from the whiteboard, e.g. *dolly*.
- The first child throws the ball to another child who says the first letter of the word, e.g. 'd'.
- They throw the ball to another child who says the next letter, e.g. 'o'.
- This continues until the final child says 'y' (pronounced 'y' as in *dolly*). This child throws it one last time to another child, who says the whole word, i.e. *dolly*.
- Explain that if the children are too slow then they will be out and will have to sit down. If the word being spelled out becomes too slow, it may need to be restarted so that it flows clearly.
- Cross out words that have been used so that different words are chosen each time.
- Continue until there are only a few children left standing.
- This game can be repeated several times.

Activity 2: Jumble me up

- Give the children a copy of the Jumble me up resource (see You will need).
- Explain to the children that today their challenge is to jumble and unjumble words using the 'y' sound.
- Show them the first flower on the Jumble me up resource. Explain that the sound that we are learning – 'y' – must go in the centre of the flower.
- Tell them that you have used all the letters from one of this week's words and placed one on each petal in a random order. Explain that you did this without the class looking so you did not give them any clues.
- Ask the class to tell their partner what they think the word might be.
- Write the word *windy* in the space underneath the flower.
- Explain that the children's task today is to use the word list and jumble a word up for a friend using the flower petals. Remind them that they can leave a petal blank if there are not enough letters and to only write each letter once, unless it occurs more than once.
- Encourage the children to move around the class and work with different children, swapping papers to create a secret word jumble for each other.
- Complete each word jumble before creating a new one and check each other's spelling.
- Encourage the children to look at the sheet and not to choose a word that has already been chosen by another child.

5 Review

Activity 3: Bag the 'y'

- Tell the children that today they are going to play a game to catch as many words using the 'y' sound as they can.
- Take the children to the sports hall. (If space is limited, a classroom could be used with the desks pushed to the sides and counters instead of beanbags used to make the task more challenging.)
- Give each pair of children a set of cut-out 'y' word cards (see You will need) and ask them to space them out in front of them. Ask them to take several steps back and agree a place for them to both start from.
- At this point, demonstrate by saying a word and throwing a beanbag to land on this word. If it misses the word it becomes your partner's go. If it lands correctly you can collect and keep this word.
- Continue playing the game until all the words have been collected. The child with the most words wins the game.
- Swap partners and repeat the game, placing the words in different positions.

Can you snore on the shore?

Focus: letter strings 'ore', 'are', 'ear', as in *more, bare, pear*

You will need:

Access online resources at My Rising Stars: www.risingstars-uk.com

- Silly rhymes for display
- Find the sound resource per child
- Word maker resource per group
- Whiteboards and pens

In a nutshell

Teacher subject knowledge for this unit:

These three letter word strings are called trigraphs.

Word list

ore	are	ear
more	bare	bear
score	dare	pear
before	care	wear
wore	share	swear
shore	scared	tear
bore	rare	
core	stare	
store	mare	
tore	spare	
snore		
sore		

1 Introduce/Review

- Read the poem from the Silly rhymes resource named 'The Bear with the Pear' (see You will need).
- Ask the children if they heard a repeated sound in the poem. Explain that the 'are/ear' sound is one of the sounds that they are learning this week.
- Go through the poem on the whiteboard and highlight every word that contains the 'are/ear' sound.
- Now read the three short ditties from the Silly rhymes resource and again ask the children to identify that the other sound is the 'ore' sound.
- Go through the ditties and highlight the words containing the 'ore' sound.

2 Teach

- Write the words *bare* and *bear* on the whiteboard. Sound them out with the children and underline the 'are/ear' sound in each.
- Explain that both these words contain the same sound, but they are spelled differently and mean different things. Explain that these types of word are called homophones and they will learn more about these in year 2. Explain the meaning of both words.
- Now show some words spelled using the 'are' spelling, e.g. *share, mare, stare.*
- Show some words using the 'ear' spelling, e.g. *pear, wear, swear.*
- Write the word *more* on the whiteboard and underline the 'ore' sound. Ask the children to say the sound and practise with the words *score* and *before*.

3 Practise

- Give each child a copy of the Find the sound resource (see You will need). Put the children into groups of three and ask one child to write 'ear' in the centre bubble, one child 'are' and the last child 'ore' in the centre bubble on the page so that they have a sheet for each sound.

Challenge!

Use the Spelling Fox Challenge: Can you snore on the shore? to kick off or consolidate the learning. The children must help the Spelling Fox find the correct answers! Access online via My Rising Stars.

- Display the highlighted poem 'The Bear with the Pear' and the three short ditties.
- Ask the children in their groups to take each highlighted word and write it in one of the boxes around the correct sound.
- Ask the children to work in groups to complete this task.

4 Apply

Activity 1: Silly rhymes

- Re-read the ditties from the Silly rhymes resource (see You will need).
- Demonstrate how the words that rhyme all tend to be at the end of the lines.
- Ask the children if they can come up with their own silly rhymes using the words on the sheets which they created in the previous session.
- Demonstrate this activity first using several of the words in three short sentences.
- Tell the children to start with just one set of words and to use as many of the words as they can.
- Ask the children to orally compose their rhymes. Tablets could be used to record the group's work and play it back for the class.

Activity 2: Word maker

- In groups, give the children one of the sets of letters from the Word maker resource (see You will need).
- Ask the group to cut out the letters.
- Challenge them to create as many words as they can using just these letters.
- Ask the groups to write their words in their spelling journals or on whiteboards.
- Swap sets of letters so that each group has a chance to work with each set.
- Feed back which words each group has made and check for accurate spelling.

5 Review

- Put the class into groups.
- Display the list of words from the 'Teach' session on the whiteboard, adding to it with extra words from the word list.
- Give each child a whiteboard and ask them to divide their boards into three sections. Ask them to write 'ore' in one section, 'are' in another section and 'ear' in the last section.
- Explain that their challenge is to listen to a word and decide which spelling/sound it uses and to be the first person to find the correct sound.
- Demonstrate this activity by taking turns to choose a word and then saying it out loud. When all of the groups have made their choice, demonstrate looking at the original word and checking who has got it right.
- Swap roles and continue completing as many words as possible.
- Swap groups so children can play with different partners.

Can you give me a word?

Focus: revision of sounds from units 4–8, Spring term

You will need:

Access online resources at My Rising Stars: www.risingstars-uk.com

- Revision word cards cut out
- Bag
- Give me a word playing board per group
- Counters and dice

In a nutshell

Teacher subject knowledge for this unit:

Revision of sounds learned in units 4–8.

1 Introduce/Review

- Tell the children that this week they are going to use in their spelling some of the sounds that they learned last term.
- Cut out the Revision word cards (see You will need) and place them in a bag.
- Pass the bag around the circle and chant the rhyme:

  We are learning how to spell.
  We can do it very well.
  We are looking for a sound.
  Is this the word in which it's found?

- At the end of the rhyme, the child holding the bag picks a card and reads the word. The whole class checks the word and then together sounds it out using the digraph/sound in the word.
- Remind the children of the digraph/sound in this word and ask if they can remember any other word using the same sound. Help them recall at least two other words in this family. Write these under the sound/digraph heading on the whiteboard.
- Repeat with all the remaining words.
- At the end of this activity draw the children's attention to the digraphs used and read the words together.

2 Teach

- Remind the children of all the digraphs that they found and remembered in the previous session.
- Recap each of the digraphs, checking children know how to pronounce them and say them correctly.
- The digraphs to revise are 'ff', 'll', 'ss', 'zz', 'ck', 'ar', 'or', 'ow/ou', 'oa/ow' and 'er/ur'.
- For each digraph give an example and ask the children to help you sound it out and write it on the whiteboard.
- Encourage the children to recall other examples that use the same spelling.
- Ask pairs to use one or more of the words and orally compose a sentence that uses this word.

3 Practise

Activity 1: Hangman

- Make sure the words from the previous session are available for the children to see. First, ask the children to work with those words displayed, but explain that they can challenge themselves and their partners by using others with the same sound.
- In pairs the children play hangman.
- Ask one child to come to the front of the class and to choose a word from the board. Ask this child to draw a dash for each letter in their chosen word. As a class demonstrate guessing letters that might be in the word.

Challenge!

Use the Spelling Fox Challenge: Can you give me a word? to kick off or consolidate the learning. The children must help the Spelling Fox find the correct answers! Access online via My Rising Stars.

- Demonstrate how the child should write the letters guessed and how to draw a hangman with each wrong guess.
- Ask the children to complete this activity in pairs.
- Swap and repeat.

4 Apply

Activity 2: Give me a word

- Show the children the Give me a word playing board from the resources (see You will need).
- Demonstrate taking turns to roll the dice and moving the counter the correct number of spaces.
- Explain that each square will give them a challenge which they need to complete using their knowledge of the digraphs/sounds from last term.
- Children complete the game in groups of three or four.
- Children can record the words in the game on whiteboards or in their spelling journals.
- Explain that they can use their spelling journals and any word lists as support but if they cannot think of the answer or get the answer wrong then they must put their counter back on the square they started on at the start of their turn.
- The first player to reach the end of the game wins.
- Repeat the game but play with different partners.
- Children are likely to land on different squares each time they play the game.

5 Review

- Dictate the following sentences for the class to write in their spelling journals:

  The girl was in love with the chief.
  They have to give him a good book.
  The ship was the third to sink on the sandbank.
  There are lots of birds in the field.

Can you find a pair?

Focus: revision of sounds from units 9–12, Spring term

You will need:

Access online resources at My Rising Stars: www.risingstars-uk.com

- Revision word cards cut out
- Bag
- Dictate me a sentence cards cut out per group
- Revision word search per child

In a nutshell

Teacher subject knowledge for this unit:

Revision of sounds learned in units 9–12.

1 Introduce/Review

- Tell the children that this week they are going to use in their spelling some of the sounds that they learned last term.
- Cut out the word cards from the Revision word cards resource (see You will need) and place them in a bag.
- Pass the bag around the circle and chant the rhyme:

  We are learning how to spell.
  We can do it very well.
  We are looking for a sound.
  Is this the word in which it's found?

- At the end of the rhyme, the child holding the bag picks a card and reads the word. The whole class checks the word and then together sounds it out using the digraph/sound in the word.
- Remind the children of the digraph/sound in this word and ask if they can remember any other word using the same sound. Help them recall at least two other words in this family. Write these under the sound/digraph headings on the whiteboard.
- Repeat with all the remaining words.

2 Teach

- Remind the children of all the digraphs that they found and remembered in the previous session.
- Recap each of the digraphs, checking children know how to pronounce them and say them correctly.
- For each digraph give an example and ask the children to help you sound it out and write it on the whiteboard.

3 Practise

- Display the words from Revision word cards resource and the words written in the first session.
- Ask the children to work in pairs. One child should choose a word and their partner needs to orally compose a sentence that uses this word.
- Demonstrate this and remind the class that the word should make sense in the sentence they create.
- Ask the pairs to feed back to the class with the best sentence that they composed. The class could be challenged to guess which word in the sentence was the one that the child was given to use.

4 Apply

Activity 1: Pairs

- Give groups of children two copies of the words from the Revision word cards resource.
- Explain to the class that the task is to find and read the matching cards.

Challenge!

Use the Spelling Fox Challenge: Can you find a pair? to kick off or consolidate the learning. The children must help the Spelling Fox find the correct answers! Access online via My Rising Stars.

- Demonstrate muddling up the cards, turning them over face down and spreading them out over the floor or table.
- Explain that on their turn they can only flip over two cards and if they can read them and they match then they get to keep them.
- Explain that if they need help reading the word then they cannot keep them, even if they match, but that they can try again on their next turn.
- If they do not match, remind the children to place them back in their original positions and encourage them to try to remember where they were for when they might find a correct match.
- Continue playing the game until all the pairs have been found.

Activity 2: Dictate me a sentence

- Give pairs of children the cut-out sentences from the Dictate me a sentence resource (see You will need).
- Read the sentences as a class, ensuring that the children know what they say and how to pronounce all the words.
- Explain that today the children are going to be the teachers and are going to dictate a sentence to their partner to write.
- Demonstrate turning the sentences face down, choosing one and dictating this to a child to write.
- Demonstrate checking the sentence using the original sentence as support.
- Remind the children that they need to correct their sentences if there are errors.

5 Review

Activity 3: Word search

- Show the children the Revision word search resource (see You will need).
- Explain that each word can only go in one direction: horizontal, vertical or diagonal.
- Demonstrate how to find the first word, how to colour it and cross it off the list at the bottom of the page.

t	e	e	w	c	g	h	w	n	e
z	e	e	r	h	z	t	h	i	f
j	a	b	e	a	e	d	i	h	a
r	s	d	a	g	h	r	l	p	s
a	i	a	t	h	o	s	e	l	t
r	h	o	p	e	p	h	q	o	u
f	a	j	m	g	a	l	m	d	n
b	i	e	m	p	i	g	a	z	e
t	h	v	p	e	r	o	c	s	v
t	w	y	e	x	p	m	s	g	c

Can you help the friends walk home?

Focus: common exception words

You will need:

Access online resources at My Rising Stars: www.risingstars-uk.com

- Exception cards cut out per group
- Bag
- Magnetic letters and boards or mini sticky notes
- Help the friends playing board per pair
- Dice and counters
- Whiteboards and pens

In a nutshell

Teacher subject knowledge for this unit:

This week focuses on words which are not phonetically decodable. Generally the grapheme-phoneme correspondences do not fit in with what has been taught so far. Children need to be taught to learn these words in different ways and to become familiar with them by sight.

Word list

love	full	school	ask
one	come	push	house
friend	once	some	pull
put			

1 Introduce/Review

- Explain that this week you are looking at exception words. Ask the children if they can remember why these words are different (i.e. they are not spelled how they sound).
- Put the cut-out Exception cards resource (see You will need) into a bag and have the children sit in a circle.
- Tell the children that they are going to go on an 'exception hunt'. Explain that they need to help search for the tricky exception words. Tell them that these words have become muddled up with words that are easy to sound out phonetically and their task is to sort them out and find the exception words.
- Demonstrate selecting a card without looking and then sounding it out. Ask the children whether it makes sense. If it does then it is not an exception word and can be kept in a separate pile. If it is an exception word then the card is kept on the floor in the middle of the circle.
- Pass the bag around the circle and as a class all say the following chant:

  We are going on a word hunt.
  Can we find an exception word?
  Let's stop and look around.
  Have we found a tricky one?

- At the end of the rhyme, the child holding the bag selects a card.
- Continue until the class has sorted all the cards.
- Keep the exception cards that have been found for the next session.

2 Teach

- Remind the children that this week they are learning new common exception words.
- Write on the whiteboard *push*. Try to sound it out and demonstrate that it does not follow normal phoneme sounds.
- Write the words *put*, *pull* and *full* and ask the children to sound these out with a partner and explain to their partner why they are tricky words. (These words are exception words since the grapheme-phoneme correspondence does not fit with what has been taught so far.)
- Highlight the similar sounds in these words and remind the children how they can learn one of the words and use it to help them learn the rest.
- Now write the words *love*, *come* and *some* on the whiteboard and repeat the paired work.
- Repeat for *one* and *once*.
- Show the children the remaining four words that they need to learn this week: *ask*, *friend*, *school* and *house*.

> **Challenge!**
> Use the Spelling Fox Challenge: Can you help the friends walk home? to kick off or consolidate the learning. The children must help the Spelling Fox find the correct answers! Access online via My Rising Stars.

- Explain to the children that there are different ways they can learn tricky words, and demonstrate sounding out 's-ch-oo-l' and learning to spell it phonetically.
- Ask the children to choose one of these words and decide with a partner how they can learn this word.
- Take feedback from the children for each of the words, highlighting any different methods that the children have used.

3 Practise

Activity 1: Magnetic words

- Give small groups of children a set of magnetic letters and a set of Exception word cards from the resources.
- Ask one child from the group to choose a card and, without showing the group, read it out. The rest of the group together makes this word using the magnetic letters. The first child then checks the word and corrects it if necessary.
- The children swap roles and continue until all the words have been spelled out using the magnetic letters. (Alternatively, mini sticky notes could be used with the required letters.)

4 Apply

Activity 2: Help the friends walk home from school

- Tell the children that today they need to help the friends walk home from school.
- Give pairs of children the Help the friends playing board from the resources (see You will need), counters and a dice.
- Demonstrate rolling the dice and moving a counter from the start of the board (the school) the correct number of squares.
- Tell the children that they then need to say the word correctly and their partner needs to check that it is correct. Once they have said the word together they need to orally compose a sentence that uses this word.
- Explain to the children that if they get the word correct they can stay where they are, but if they get it wrong they must move back to the square where they started their turn.
- Pairs of children play the game, continuing until one player reaches home.
- This activity can be repeated with children landing on different squares.

Activity 3: School's started!

- Remind the children of the game they played in Activity 2.
- Explain to them that the school bell has rung and the friends need to get to school before the teacher finishes taking the register.
- Explain that this time their counters will start at home and follow the route back to school.
- Explain that this time when they land on a square they need to say the word correctly, cover it over and then write it correctly. Demonstrate this and ask a child to check your spelling, comparing it to the word on the game board.
- Explain to the children that if they get the word correct they can stay where they are, but if they get it wrong they must move back to the square where they started their turn.
- Pairs of children play the game, continuing until one player reaches school.
- This activity can be repeated with children landing on different squares.

5 Review

- Dictate the following sentences to the class for the children to write on whiteboards or in their spelling journals:

  I come to school once a day.
  My friend walks to my house.
  If someone comes you must hide.
  She says you must put one book down.

Can you help The Kind Witch?

Focus: letter string 'tch', as in *catch, fetch, kitchen*

You will need:

Access online resources at My Rising Stars: www.risingstars-uk.com

- The Kind Witch story for display
- Spelling roll playing board per child
- Word cards – 'tch' sound cut out, enough for one per child
- Dice and colouring pencils

In a nutshell

Teacher subject knowledge for this unit:

The /tʃ/ sound is usually spelled as 'tch' if it comes straight after a single short vowel letter. Some exceptions to this are the words *rich, which, much, such.*

Word list

catch	hutch	witch	match
fetch	latch	stitch	ketchup
notch	snatch	crutch	butcher

1 Introduce/Review

- Tell the children that they have a new sound to learn this week and that you have a story to read them that uses this new sound.
- Read the story The Kind Witch (see You will need).
- Ask the children if they heard any repeated sound that they think might be what they are learning this week. Explain that there is a big clue in the title.
- Explain that the sound they are learning is the 'tch' sound.
- Tell the children you will read the story again and ask them to put their thumbs up when they hear the 'tch' sound.
- Display the story and as you read it, stop and highlight any word that uses the 'tch' sound.
- Ask the children to read the story together in pairs using the highlighted board version.
- Ask the children to help you make a list of the 'tch' words used in a spider diagram for display on the working wall.

2 Teach

- Look at the spider diagram from the last session and remind children that this week they are learning the 'tch' sound.
- Explain that the 'tch' sound is usually spelled with a 't-c-h' when it comes after a single short vowel. Remind children of the short vowel sounds *a*, *e*, *i*, *o* and *u*.
- Demonstrate this spelling with the words *notch*, *hutch*, *latch* and *fetch*.
- Explain to the class that the 'tch' sound can appear in the middle of the word, for example *ketchup* and *butcher*.
- Write the words *rich*, *which*, *much* and *such* on the whiteboard. Ask the children what is different about these words. Explain that these are the words that do not follow the pattern and they do not have the 't' with the 'ch'. Leave these words visible for the children during the week's activities.

3 Practise

- Give the children a Spelling roll playing board each (see You will need). Display the words from the word list on the whiteboard or use the words created during the first session.
- Tell the children that they need to write one word in each box. All the words that they write should contain the sound 'tch'. They should try to use all the words in the word list and each column should contain different words.
- Explain that by writing the words it will help them practise the spellings and that they will use their completed sheets next lesson.

Challenge!

Use the Spelling Fox Challenge: Can you help The Kind Witch? to kick off or consolidate the learning. The children must help the Spelling Fox find the correct answers! Access online via My Rising Stars.

4 Apply

Activity 1: Spelling roll

- Give the children their filled in playing boards from the last session.
- Tell the children that they are going to play 'Spelling roll' using their playing boards.
- Model how to play the game with a child. Roll the dice and demonstrate that if it lands on number 4 your partner reads out (from your own playing board) the first word in the fourth column for you to write on a whiteboard. Ask your partner to check your spelling using your playing board. If it is correct, you can colour in that word on your playing board. (Children could alternatively place a counter over the word they have spelled correctly.)
- Your partner then rolls the dice and you take their playing board ready to read out the relevant word. Remind children to each use a different colour.
- The first person to complete one column on their playing board wins the game.

Activity 2: Roll race!

- Explain that this is played very much like Activity 1 but in this game it is a race to spell the words correctly.
- This may need modelling at the front of the class before the activity begins.
- Give groups of three children a filled in playing board that hasn't been coloured.
- One child rolls the dice and reads the first uncoloured word in that column number.
- The other two children now race to be the first to write the word on their whiteboards correctly.
- The first child checks the spelling and the child that answered fastest with the correct spelling colours in that word on the playing board. The children swap roles and continue, each colouring words that they have won in different colours.
- If the dice is rolled and the column is completely filled, the child can choose to ask any uncoloured word on the board.
- Continue until the board is completely coloured and the child with the most coloured squares wins the game.

5 Review

Activity 3: Fetch the witch!

- Remind the class of the words from the word list and sound them out together. Ensure the children can say all of the words.
- Tell the class that you are going to play 'Fetch the witch!'. In this game the witch is trying to find the person who has stolen her homemade butterscotch. Use the 'tch' word cards (see You will need).
- Explain that one person will be given the word *witch* and they need to go out of the room and wait until they are called in.
- Explain that you will give each child a word card and they need to make sure they can say their word and then hide it behind their back. Some children will have the same word.
- Explain that one child will be given the word *butterscotch*.
- When the witch comes back into the room they need to ask a child:

  What have you hidden in the flower patch?

- The child then needs to say their word after the reply *I have hidden ...* .
- The witch has three guesses to find the butterscotch. If they guess correctly they have another go; if they do not, the child with butterscotch then becomes the witch.
- The game continues with the children being given different words.

Can you help Tim make plurals?

Focus: adding 's' and 'es' to words, as in *cats, catches*

You will need:

Access online resources at My Rising Stars: www.risingstars-uk.com

- Write my plural resource per group
- This is Tim resource for display
- Plural reminder bubble resource for display
- Plural cards cut out per pair
- Whiteboards and pens

In a nutshell

Teacher subject knowledge for this unit:

A suffix is a letter or group of letters added to the end of a word to change its meaning. To make the word plural, or to describe an action someone else is doing, we usually add 's' to the end. If the ending of a word is 's', 'x', 'z', 'ch' or 'sh', we add 'es', which forms an extra syllable or beat and makes the ending sound like /ɪz/ and e.g. *catches*.

Word list

s		es	
cats	rugs	catches	pushes
dogs	bags	buses	crashes
spends	hills	boxes	brushes
rocks	plums	kisses	foxes
thanks	sleeps	misses	
cards	wears	churches	
words	sings	dishes	
hats	plays	bosses	
pens	falls	misses	
kings	says	wishes	
boys	hits	teaches	

1 Introduce/Review

- Explain to the class that for the next two weeks they will be learning how to change the meaning of a word by adding 's' or 'es' to the end.
- Give groups of children the set of cut-out cards from the Write my plural resource (see You will need).
- Ask the groups to take turns in choosing a card and then to write the plural version of the word underneath the picture. Encourage the groups to work together with each card before moving on to the next picture.
- Go through the pictures and words and check that the children have written the words correctly, adding an 's'.
- Now show the children the picture of the boy 'Tim' on the This is Tim resource (see You will need).
- Ask the class to think of two things that Tim could be doing, e.g. swimming.
- Ask the class to help you complete the four bubbles underneath the picture of Tim, describing what he is doing. Write *Tim swims, Tim sings* etc.
- The class could write these on their own whiteboards to reinforce their learning.

2 Teach

- Remind children of the work they completed in the previous session.
- Explain that for many objects (nouns), to make them plural (where there is more than one of them) you only need to add an 's'. Go through the cards from the Write my plural resource and ask the children to say them in their plural form with you.
- Now remind the children of Tim from the This is Tim resource and explain that when someone is doing something (a verb), we also need to add an 's' to make the sentence correct.

Challenge!

Use the Spelling Fox Challenge: Can you help Tim make plurals? to kick off or consolidate the learning. The children must help the Spelling Fox find the correct answers! Access online via My Rising Stars.

- Now write *fox* and *foxes* on the whiteboard. Ask the children what you have added to make *fox* plural. Underline the 'es' to highlight the additional letters.
- Explain that where a word ends with an 's', 'x', 'z', 'ch' or 'sh' sound, they cannot just add an 's', they have to add an 'es'.
- Show the class the Plural reminder bubble from the resources (see You will need) and say the sounds together as a class. Display this on the working wall.
- Say the word *kiss*. Ask the class if this word ends in one of the sounds in the reminder bubble. Go through the sounds and demonstrate that it has the 's' sound at the end. Ask the class to help you make it into a plural, demonstrating that you add 'es'.
- Now say the word *kiss* and clap the syllable. Say the word *kisses* and clap the two syllables. Explain that when you make this word into a plural, it forms an extra syllable, and this shows that it must use 'es' at the end.

3 Practise

- Write the word *bus* on the whiteboard. Remind the class to use the Plural reminder bubble and decide if it ends in any of the endings that are in the bubble. Ask the class to write the plural form on their whiteboards or in their spelling journals. Take feedback from the class, demonstrating that it uses the ending 'es'.
- Ask the children to clap the syllables in *bus* and *buses*. Ask the class if the plural form creates an extra syllable and establish that it does and hence uses the 'es' ending.
- Continue this with the words *box*, *catch*, *church* and *wish*.

4 Apply

Activity 1: Clap my syllables

- Give pairs of children the set of cut-out cards from the Plural cards resource (see You will need).
- Explain that the cards show words with only one syllable.
- Explain that when they add the plural ending, some of the words will become two syllables and some will stay as only one syllable. Remind the class how to do this with *cat/cats* and *fox/foxes*.
- Ask the class in their pairs to choose a card, clap the syllable, then make it plural and clap the syllable(s) again. If it changes into two syllables, ask them to put it in one pile and if it does not change to put it in another pile.
- Look at the two piles the pairs have made and check as a class.
- Remind the class that the pile of words that have two syllables as a plural have 'es' as an ending and the single syllable pile only have an 's'.

Activity 2: Give me an ending

- Remind the class of Activity 1 and ask them to use the same cards in their pairs.
- Display the Plural reminder bubble and remind the class how to use this to help them.
- Ask pairs to choose a card, write the word in their spelling journals, decide whether to add 's' or 'es' and then write the plural form. Demonstrate this for clarity.
- Remind the class that they can use the reminder bubble together with their syllable clapping that they practised in Activity 1 to support their work.

5 Review

- Dictate the following sentences for the children to write in their spelling journals:

  My friend likes school.
  I had some plums for my snack.
  She wishes to see some dolphins.
  The horses were still like rocks.

Can you help the dog and the fox?

Focus: adding 's' and 'es' to words, as in *cats, catches*

You will need:

Access online resources at My Rising Stars: www.risingstars-uk.com

- Plural word cards cut out
- Bag
- Blue and red colouring pencils
- Write the plural cards resource, cut out
- Dogs or foxes? resource per child
- Dictate me plural sentences cut out, per pair

In a nutshell

Teacher subject knowledge for this unit:

A suffix is a letter or group of letters added to the end of a word to change its meaning. If the ending of a word is 's', 'x', 'z', 'ch' or 'sh' it is spelled with an *-es* for the plural. If the ending sounds like /ɪz/ and forms an extra syllable or 'beat' in the word the plural is spelled with an *-es*.

Word list

s		es	
cats	rugs	catches	pushes
dogs	bags	buses	crashes
spends	hills	boxes	brushes
rocks	plums	kisses	foxes
thanks	sleeps	misses	
cards	wears	churches	
words	sings	dishes	
hats	plays	bosses	
pens	falls	misses	
kings	says	wishes	
boys	hits	teaches	

1 Introduce/Review

- Display the Plural reminder bubble from the previous week on the whiteboard.
- Cut out the cards from the Plural word cards resource (see You will need) and place them in a bag.
- Ask the children to sit in a circle and pass the bag around the circle to the following chant:

  We are learning how to spell.
  We can do it very well.
  's' or 'es', which will it be?
  Time to stop, is it me?

- At the end of the rhyme the child holding the bag chooses a word and reads it out.
- Ask the rest of the class whether this word uses the 's' or 'es' ending. Remind the class to use the reminder bubble as support. The class claps the syllables together and decides if it has one ('s' ending) or two ('es' ending).
- Repeat with the remainder of the cards.

2 Teach

- Remind the children of the previous activity.
- Remind the class that if adding the ending does not make an extra syllable then they only need to add the letter 's'. If it does add an extra syllable then they need to add 'es' on to the word.
- Give the class some examples of words and ask them to clap the syllables. Reminding them whether the word uses the 's' or 'es' ending.
- Show the class the Plural reminder bubble from the previous week and ask them to say the sounds 's', 'z', 'x', 'sh' and 'ch'. Remind them that if the root word ends in one of these sounds then they need to add 'es' rather than 's'.

Challenge!

Use the Spelling Fox Challenge: Can you help the dog and the fox? to kick off or consolidate the learning. The children must help the Spelling Fox find the correct answers! Access online via My Rising Stars.

3 Practise

- Give pairs of children a copy of the Write the plural resource cut-out cards (see You will need).
- Ask the pairs to work together to write the plural of the item shown on the card under each picture.
- When finished ask them to sort the cards into those that use the 's' and those that use the 'es' ending.
- Ask the pairs to check their spelling and sorting with another pair, correcting any errors with the teacher's help.

4 Apply

Activity 1: Dog or fox?

- Explain to the children that a dog and a fox each had some balloons. The dog's balloons were blue and the fox's balloons were red, but they have become muddled and rain has washed the colours away.
- Explain to the children that luckily the balloons had words on them. The dog had balloons with words that the plural form ends in just an 's', like the plural of *dogs*. The fox had balloons with words that the plural form ends in an 'es', like the plural of *foxes*.
- Show the children Dogs or foxes? resource (see You will need) and explain that they need to cut out the pictures of the dog and the fox and stick them each on separate pages in their spelling journals.
- They then need to cut out each balloon, make it into a plural by adding an 's' or 'es' and stick it with either the dog or the fox, depending on the ending of the word.
- When they have finished they can check their work with a partner and give the balloons back their colour – blue for the dog and red for the fox.

Activity 2: Sentence maker

- Give the children back their work from Activity 1.
- Ask the children to work in pairs. One child should choose a word on one of the balloons and their partner then needs to orally compose a sentence that uses this word.
- Demonstrate this and remind the class that the word should make sense in the sentence they create.
- Ask the pairs to feed back to the class with the best sentence that they composed.
- The class could be challenged to then jointly compose a final sentence which uses two of the words, e.g. *says* and *catches (He says that he catches fish with his hat!)*

5 Review

Activity 3: Dictate me a sentence

- Give pairs of children the cut-out sentences from the Dictate me plural sentences resource (see You will need).
- Read the sentences as a class, ensuring that the children know what they say and how to pronounce all the words.
- Explain that today the children are going to be the teachers and are going to dictate a sentence to their partner to write.
- Demonstrate turning the sentences face down, choosing one and dictating this to a child to write.
- Demonstrate checking the sentence using the original sentence as support.
- Remind the children that they need to correct their sentences if there are errors.

Can you help the animals by adding *-ing*?

Focus: adding *-ing*, as in *hunting, buzzing, jumping*

You will need:

Access online resources at My Rising Stars: www.risingstars-uk.com

- Playing Friends poem for display
- Create my poem resource per child
- Blank grid resource per child, if required
- Search for *-ing* word search resource per child

In a nutshell

Teacher subject knowledge for this unit:

Adding the suffix *-ing* always adds an extra syllable to the word.
If the verb ends in two consonant letters (the same or different), the ending is simply added on.

Word list

hunting	stealing	heating	honking
buzzing	sinking	waiting	waiting
jumping	crying	thinking	roaring
tweeting	playing	adding	eating
splashing	meeting	crashing	learning
growling	lighting	tearing	
blowing	flying	crawling	

1 Introduce/Review

- Tell the children that this week they are learning to add suffixes on to words. Explain that a suffix is a group of letters that you can add on to the end of a word to change the meaning of the word.
- Explain that you have a poem to read them called 'Playing Friends' and they need to listen out to try to spot how the endings of the words are similar.
- Display the Playing Friends poem (see You will need) and read the poem to the class.
- Take comments from the class and explain that this week they are learning to add *-ing* on to the end of words.
- Ask the class to tell a partner some words that use the *-ing* suffix. Take some feedback from the class and ask them to see if they hear or spot any of these whilst you re-read the poem.
- Go through the poem and highlight the *-ing* from each word.
- Ask the class to discuss with a pair other doing words (verbs) that could have *-ing* on the end.
- Tell the class that their task is to find words that just need *-ing* added on to the end and do not need any change to the root word. Explain that you will write on the whiteboard any verbs that do not require the root word to change, e.g. *snowing*, but they should offer you their ideas.
- Display the highlighted poem on the working wall.

2 Teach

- Write the words *meet* and *meeting* on the whiteboard.
- Ask the children to clap the syllables in each word and explain that an extra syllable is always added by the *-ing*. Demonstrate this with two more examples, e.g. *buzzing, crying*.
- Ask the children what happened to the root word, i.e. the word *meet*, when it became *meeting*.
- Explain that in all the words that they are using this week, the root word does not change and all that happens is that *-ing* is added on to the end.
- Ask the children to help you add *-ing* on to *catch, crash* and *tear*.

Challenge!

Use the Spelling Fox Challenge: Can you help the animals by adding *-ing*? to kick off or consolidate the learning. The children must help the Spelling Fox find the correct answers! Access online via My Rising Stars.

3 Practise

- Remind the class of the poem from the resources, Playing Friends (see You will need).
- Show the class the Create my poem resource (see You will need) and ask them to complete the poem in their own way using words ending in *-ing*.
- Check that the children can read all the words in the word list and understand the meaning.
- Explain to the children that they have two word lists for the poem, one with *-ing*. verbs and one with animals. Ask them to complete the gaps with either a verb or an animal.
- Explain that for the final two lines they need to choose both a verb and an animal to complete their poem.
- Encourage the children to use the suggested verbs or verbs that were written on the whiteboard in the first session, i.e. where the root word does not change by adding *-ing*.
- Ask the children to share their poems with a partner.

4 Apply

Activity 1: Write it right

- Tell the children that today they are going to try to write some *-ing* verbs right (correctly) in playing the game 'Write it right'.
- Give each child the Blank grid resource (see You will need) and ask them to cut out the squares.
- Display the word list created in the first session and the highlighted poem from the Playing Friends poem resource.
- Ask the children to write six different words that use the *-ing* ending. Encourage them to copy the words to get the spelling correct.
- Demonstrate playing the game with a partner by turning the cards created from both players face down, muddled up and spread out on the floor or table.
- The first player chooses a card and reads what it says without showing their partner.
- Their partner now needs to write the word on their whiteboard or in their spelling journal.
- They then show their work and the first child checks that the word is spelled correctly.
- If it is correct then it can be kept by the child who has written the word. If it is incorrect then it is placed back down with the rest of the cards.
- The game continues until all the cards have been claimed.
- Keep the cards for use in Activity 2.

Activity 2: Doing words

- Remind the children that all the words that they are learning this week are verbs or 'doing words'.
- Explain that they are going to play a guessing game.
- Demonstrate choosing a word from the cards created in Activity 1 and tell the children that you cannot tell them what the card says but they have to try to guess from what you are about to do.
- Explain that the child who gets it correct can have the next turn.
- Now act out the word on the card, e.g. *crying*, and encourage the children to guess what you are doing.
- Encourage the children to act silently so as to not give away the word. Remind the class that they must guess using the *-ing* endings.
- Put the class into groups, with a selection of cards from Activity 2, to play the game.

5 Review

Activity 3: Word search

- Show the children the word search from the Searching for *-ing* resource (see You will need).
- Explain that each word can only go in one direction: horizontal, vertical or diagonal.
- Demonstrate how to find the first word, how to colour it and cross it off the list at the bottom of the page.
- Ask the children to complete the word search.

Can you find a path through the river?

Focus: adding *-ed*, as in *hunted, buzzed, jumped*

You will need:

Access online resources at My Rising Stars: www.risingstars-uk.com

- Mark my homework for display
- *-ed* cards cut out per group
- Roll 'n' write instructions for display
- Roll 'n' write my way for groups
- Path through the river per child
- Path through the river (answers) for display

In a nutshell

Teacher subject knowledge for this unit:

Adding the suffix *-ed* sometimes adds an extra syllable to the word.
The past tense of some verbs may sound as if it ends in /ɪd/ (extra syllable), /d/ or /t/ (no extra syllable), but all these endings are spelled 'ed', e.g. *buzzed, jumped.*
If the verb ends in two consonant letters (the same or different), the ending is simply added on.

Word list

hunted	splashed	heated	crashed
buzzed	growled	waited	roared
jumped	snowed	played	crawled
twisted	honked	added	hunted

1 Introduce/Review

- Tell the children that you were very busy last night doing your homework. Your task was to make sure the sentences you wrote made sense using the correct verb (doing word).
- Display the Mark my homework resource (see You will need) and ask the children to help you look at the sentences and check that the verbs you have written are correct.
- Highlight the verb in each case and ask the children if the sentence makes sense. Ask the class to suggest how you could change the verb so the sentence reads correctly. Amend the ending of the verb on the whiteboard.
- Some of the verbs can be changed without adding *-ed* to make the sentence correct, e.g. *the frog jumps to get away*. In this situation encourage the children to think of another verb tense to use. Alternatively, you could add the different ending and then review the work afterwards, highlighting the *-ed* on the end of the other verbs. Then encourage the children to help make all the verbs into the same tense using the same ending, going back to correct the different ending verbs.
- Give the class a verb, e.g. *growl*, and ask the children in pairs to orally compose a sentence using the ending *-ed* for this word. Repeat with other verbs, taking feedback from pairs.

2 Teach

- Write the words *hunt* and *hunted* on the whiteboard. Clap the syllables in each and explain that, similar to the way that using *-ing* adds an extra syllable or beat to the word, the same sometimes happens when you add *-ed*.
- Repeat this with *play* and *played* (both only one syllable). Explain that adding *-ed* to a word sometimes does not add an extra syllable.
- Write the sentence *I play with my friends* and explain that this shows you are doing this now. Now write *I played with my friends* and explain that adding *-ed* on to the end of *play* shows that this happened in the past and is not happening now. Explain that all of the verbs that we are writing this week are in the past tense and will use the ending *-ed*.
- Highlight and remind the class that, like last week, in the words we are learning the root word does not change and *-ed* is simply added onto the end of the word.

Challenge!

Use the Spelling Fox Challenge: Can you find a path through the river? to kick off or consolidate the learning. The children must help the Spelling Fox find the correct answers! Access online via My Rising Stars.

3 Practise

- Show the class the *-ed* cards resource (see You will need) and read them together as a class, checking that the children can pronounce them and know what they all mean.
- Give groups of children a set of the cards and tell them to spread them out face down on the floor or table in front of them.
- Children take it in turns to choose a card and orally compose a sentence using this word. Encourage the rest of the group to support and help the child and to give feedback as to whether the sentence makes sense or could be improved.

4 Apply

Activity 1: Roll 'n' write

- Give groups of children the word cards from the *-ed* cards resource.
- Display the Roll 'n' write instructions (see You will need) and explain how the children need to write with each dice number.
- One child chooses a word at random from the set of cards. All children have a chance to look at the word and sound it out together as a group.
- The word is then turned face down and a different child rolls the dice.
- The group then writes the word in the way the dice tells them.
- The word is then turned over and the children check their spelling.
- The game continues until all the cards have been used.

Activity 2: Roll 'n' write my way

- Explain that this game is played in exactly the same way as Activity 1, but with one difference.
- Ask each group to decide how they will write the words on each roll of the dice. Encourage them to be creative, e.g. write in spiky letters, write in tiny letters, write in dotted letters.
- The group writes an example of each way they have chosen on the Roll 'n' write my way resource (see You will need).
- The group then plays the game exactly like Activity 1.

5 Review

Activity 3: Path through the river

- Show the children the Path through the river resource (see You will need) and explain that they need to cross the river using the stepping stones.
- Tell them that they cannot step on a word that does not use the past tense *-ed* ending, otherwise they will sink into the fast-flowing river and be swept away.
- Demonstrate how to start on the starting stone and to sound out the words on the stones that are next to this stone. Explain that they cannot jump over stones. Demonstrate colouring in the stone with the next *-ed* word and explain how they then continue until they find the path all the way over the river to reach the end.
- Children can compare the path that they have found to check their spelling.

Can you make new words?

Focus: adding *-er* and *-est* to adjectives, as in *grander, grandest*

You will need:

Access online resources at My Rising Stars: www.risingstars-uk.com

- Root word cards cut out
- Bag
- Sorting word cards cut out per pair
- Suffix addition per child

In a nutshell

Teacher subject knowledge for this unit:

Adding the suffixes *-er* and *-est* always adds an extra syllable to the word.
If the adjective ends in two consonant letters (the same or different), the ending is simply added on.

Word list

grander	grandest	softer	softest
fresher	freshest	brighter	brightest
quicker	quickest	darker	darkest
louder	loudest	weaker	weakest
stronger	strongest	faster	fastest
taller	tallest	sweeter	sweetest
longer	longest	higher	highest
older	oldest	nearer	nearest
smarter	smartest	lighter	lightest
shorter	shortest	smaller	smallest

1 Introduce/Review

- Ask the children to sit in a circle and place the cut-out cards from the resources, Root word cards, in a bag (see You will need).
- Write '*er*' and 'est' on the whiteboard and ask the class to practise saying these. Explain that this week the class is learning to add the suffixes *-er* and *-est* to the end of words.
- Pass the bag around the circle to the following rhyme:
  Pass the bag, one by one.
  Find a word and have some fun!
  Make new words and beat the rest.
  Just add -er and just add -est!
- When the rhyme is finished the child holding the bag takes a card out of the bag. This child then reads the card, e.g. *tall.*
- Now ask the class to add the suffix *-er* to make the word *taller* and to add the suffix *-est* to make the word *tallest*. Stick the word on the whiteboard before the letters *-er* and *-est* to visually show the new words. Ask the class to say the new words made, e.g. *taller, tallest.*
- Repeat with all the remaining cards.
- Record the new words on paper in a spider diagram around the letters *-er* and *-est* and display on the working wall.

2 Teach

- Remind the children of the two suffixes they are learning this week.
- Explain that, like last week, in the word that they are learning this week they do not need to change the root word, they simply add the suffix at the end.
- Explain that with both these suffixes an extra syllable is added to the word.
- Explain that adding *-er* makes the word mean *more* and adding *-est* means *most.*

> **Challenge!**
> Use the Spelling Fox Challenge: Can you make new words? to kick off or consolidate the learning. The children must help the Spelling Fox find the correct answers! Access online via My Rising Stars.

- Remind the class that there are special letters called vowels. Explain that all the other letters are called consonants. Write the word *fresh* on the whiteboard and underline the last two letters. Explain that these are both consonants. Explain that any word that ends with two consonants means that we do not need to change the ending of the root word before adding a suffix.
- Demonstrate this by writing *strong* on the whiteboard. Underline the two last letters and ask the children to check that these are consonants. Ask the children to confirm that we do not need to change the root word before adding the suffix.
- Repeat this for three more of the root words until the children have begun to understand this concept.

3 Practise

- Give pairs of children a set of cut-out cards from the resources, Sorting word cards (see You will need).
- Ask the pairs to sort the cards into three groups. The root words in one group, *-er* suffixes in another and all the *-est* suffixes in the final group.
- Ask the pairs to take turns to read each pile of cards out loud to each other.
- Now ask the pairs to sort the cards into six groups, putting the root word and the root word with its two linking suffixes together, e.g. *quick, quicker, quickest.*
- Challenge the children to orally compose a sentence using one word from each of the groups.

4 Apply

Activity 1: Addition sheet

- Show the children Suffix addition resource (see You will need) and explain that their task today is to add the *-er* and the *-est* endings.
- Demonstrate with the first word by adding the endings.
- Ask the children to complete the word endings on the sheet.
- Ask the children to compare their spelling with a partner and correct any errors.
- As an extension the children could orally compose sentences that use one of the *-er* or *-est* words on their sheet.

Activity 2: Snap that word

- Combine three or four groups of cut-out cards from the resources, Sorting word cards, used in the 'Practise' session.
- Deal the cards out between three and five players.
- Each player turns over a card at the same time. If the cards match, the first player to say 'snap' wins the cards from the player(s) with the matching card.
- Continue playing until all the cards have been won.
- Groups can swap around and play different children.

5 Review

- Dictate the following sentences for the children to write on whiteboards or in their spelling journals:

  My friend is the tallest in the class.
  They were nearer to the front.
  It flew higher than a bird.
  He was the oldest and the smartest in the family.

Can you help the bumblebee stinger?

Focus: adding *-er* to a verb, as in *hunter, buzzer, jumper*

You will need:

Access online resources at My Rising Stars: www.risingstars-uk.com

- The Bumblebee Stinger poem for whiteboard work
- Compose me a sentence word cards cut out per pair
- Chalk and beanbags

In a nutshell

Teacher subject knowledge for this unit:

Adding the suffix *-er* always adds an extra syllable to the word.
If the verb ends in two consonant letters (the same or different), the ending is simply added on.

Word list

hunter	worker	helper
buzzer	painter	player
jumper	cleaner	wearer
singer	teacher	spender
stinger		

1 Introduce/Review

- Read the poem 'The Bumblebee Stinger' from the resources (see You will need).
- Ask the children if they could hear a repeated sound in the poem.
- Re-read the poem and ask the children to put their thumbs up when they hear the repeated sound *-er*. Stop at each word and highlight it on the whiteboard.
- Tell the children that they are going to help you perform the poem using the *-er* words.
- Ask the children to help you create an action for each of the *-er* words. Go through the poem and decide on an action for each *-er* word.
- Once the children have decided on an action for each of the *-er* words, slowly read the poem and ask the children to help you perform it using the actions, e.g. children could pretend to hunt for treasure for *hunter*.
- Display the highlighted poem on the working wall.

2 Teach

- Remind the children that they are learning to add the suffix *-er* onto words.
- Explain that this week they are adding *-er* onto verbs (doing words) and by doing this it makes the word into a noun (an object or a person).
- Remind the children that they do not need to change the root word when the last two letters of the root word are both consonants. Demonstrate with examples *work* and *help*.
- Explain that all the words they are using this week do not need their root word changed because they all follow this rule.
- Give the class a word, e.g. *hunt*, and ask them to tell their partner what the word would be adding the suffix *-er*, i.e. *hunter*.
- Now ask the class in pairs to orally compose a sentence that uses this new word, e.g. *the hunter crept through the forest*.
- Repeat this with other words, e.g. *work, paint*.

3 Practise

Activity 1: Write it right

- Tell the children that today they are going to try to write words using the suffix *-er* right (correctly) in playing the game 'Write it right'.

Challenge!

Use the Spelling Fox Challenge: Can you help the bumblebee stinger? to kick off or consolidate the learning. The children must help the Spelling Fox find the correct answers! Access online via My Rising Stars.

- Demonstrate turning the word cards from the Compose me a sentence resource (see You will need) face down on the floor or table.
- One child chooses a card and reads what it says without showing their partner, e.g. *buzz*.
- Their partner now needs to write the word on their whiteboard or in their spelling journal, but changing the meaning and the spelling by adding the suffix *-er*, i.e. *buzzer*.
- They then show their work and the first child checks that the word is spelled correctly and that the suffix has been correctly added.
- If it is correct then it can be kept by the child who has written the word. If it is incorrect then it is placed back down with the rest of the cards.
- The game continues until all the cards have been claimed.

4 Apply

Activity 2: Compose me a sentence

- Give pairs of children the cards from the Compose me a sentence resource (see You will need).
- The pairs should spread the cards out face up in front of them. Ask them to orally compose a sentence that uses at least one of the cards but has the ending *-er*. Initially ask the children to share some of their sentences with the class.
- Once they have composed a sentence using one of the words they can collect it from the table and continue to compose a sentence using a different word(s).
- Continue composing sentences until all the words have been used by the pair.

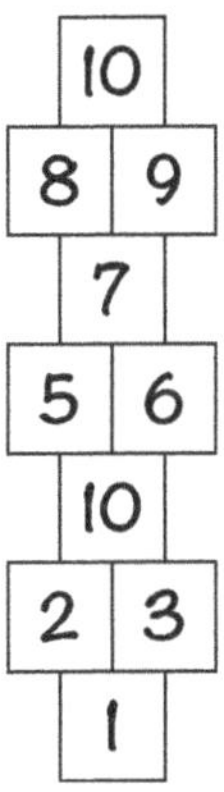

Activity 3: Word hopscotch

- Take the children outside, if weather permits, or to the sports hall.
- Divide the children into groups and use chalk to draw a hopscotch grid for each group. (Words could be written onto paper for the sports hall floor.)
- Ask the groups to write one word that uses the *-er* ending from this week's word list into each square. A word list may need to be provided.
- Show the children how to play hopscotch. Say the word on the first square and then throw a beanbag on to this square. Jump over where the beanbag lands and hop and jump on to the remaining square to the top of the grid, turn around and hop and jump back.
- Take turns to play, landing on the next square each time.
- Children swap hopscotch grids to play with a different selection of words.

5 Review

Activity 4: Turn me over?

- Give groups of children the word cards from the Compose me a sentence resource (see You will need).
- Ask the groups to take each word card and write the same root word with the *-er* ending on the opposite side.
- Complete this for each card and then lay them randomly, different ways up on the floor or table.
- Children should then take it in turns to choose a card. Once they have chosen a card they should write the word that is hidden on the opposite side on a whiteboard. They then turn it over and check their spelling. They then leave the card this way up.
- Continue playing until all the cards have been turned over twice.

Can you create some word art?

Focus: adding the prefix *un-*, as in *unhappy, undo, unload*

You will need:

Access online resources at My Rising Stars: www.risingstars-uk.com

- Root word cards cut out
- Bag
- Jumble me up resource per child
- Dictate me a sentence resource cut out per pair
- Word art designs for display

In a nutshell

Teacher subject knowledge for this unit:

A prefix is a letter or group of letters added to the start of a word to change its meaning. The prefix *un-* is added to the beginning of a word without any change to the spelling of the root word and changes the meaning of the root word to its opposite.

Word list

unhappy	unlock	unclip	unfit	unsafe
undo	unwise	unbox	unkind	untie
unload	uncut	uncover	unpack	unwise
unfair	unafraid	undid	unpin	

1 Introduce/Review

- Ask the children to sit in a circle and place the cut-out Root word cards (see You will need) in a bag.
- Write *un-* on the whiteboard and ask the class to practise saying this. Explain that this week the class is learning to add 'un' to the start of a word. Explain that this is called a prefix and helps make a different word. Explain that it is just like a suffix but added to the start and not the end.
- Pass the bag around the circle to the following rhyme:

  Pass the bag, one by one
  Today we learn the prefix, un-.
  Add to the start of each word.
  To mean the opposite of what you heard.

- When the rhyme is finished, the child holding the bag takes a card out of the bag. This child then reads the card, e.g. *happy*.
- Check that the children understand the meaning of any unfamiliar words.
- Now ask the class to add the prefix *un-* to make the opposite of the word. Stick the word on the whiteboard after the letters *un-* to visually show the new word. Ask the class to say the new word made, e.g. *unhappy*. Repeat with all the remaining cards.
- Record the new words on paper in a spider diagram around the letters *un-* and display it on the working wall.

2 Teach

- Remind the children of the prefix that they are learning to add this week.
- Explain that by adding the letters 'un' the meaning of the word is changed.
- Demonstrate this by saying that you will give one child extra playtime and asking, *Is this fair?* The class should respond that this would be *unfair*.
- Write *fair* and *unfair* on the whiteboard and underline the prefix *un-*.
- Repeat with *do*, *pack* and *safe*.
- Explain the meaning of the words if necessary.

3 Practise

Activity 1: Write it right

- Tell the children that today they are going to try to write words using the prefix *un-* right (correctly) in playing the game 'Write it right'.
- Demonstrate turning the Root word cards from the resources face down on the floor or table.

Challenge!
Use the Spelling Fox Challenge: Can you create some word art? to kick off or consolidate the learning. The children must help the Spelling Fox find the correct answers! Access online via My Rising Stars.

- One child chooses a card and reads what it says without showing their partner, e.g. *wise*.
- Their partner now needs to write the word on their whiteboard or in their spelling journal, but changing the meaning and the spelling by adding the prefix *un-*, e.g. *unwise*.
- They then show their work and the first child checks that the word is spelled correctly.
- If it is correct then it can be kept by the child who has written the word. If it is incorrect then it is placed back down with the rest of the cards.
- The game continues until all the cards have been claimed.

4 Apply

Activity 2: Jumble me up

- Give children a copy of Jumble me up (see You will need).
- Read the words in the word list as a class and check that the children can read and understand all of them.
- Explain to the children that today their challenge is to jumble and unjumble words using the 'un' sound.
- Show them the first flower on Jumble me up. Explain that the sound that they are learning, i.e. 'un', must go in the centre of the flower.
- Tell them that you have used all the letters from one of this week's words and placed one on each petal in a random order. Explain that you did this without the class looking so you did not give them any clues.
- Ask the class to tell their partner what they think the word might be.
- Write the word *unkind* in the space underneath the flower.
- Explain that the children's task today is to use the word list and jumble a word up for a friend using the flower petals. Remind them that they can leave a petal blank if there are not enough letters and to only write each letter once, unless it occurs more than once.
- Encourage the children to move around the class and work with different children, swapping papers to create a secret word jumble for each other.
- Complete each word jumble before creating a new one and check each other's spelling.
- Encourage the children to look at the sheet and not to choose a word that has already been chosen by another child.

Activity 3: Dictate me a sentence

- Give pairs of children the cut-out sentences from the Dictate me a sentence resource (see You will need).
- Read the sentences as a class, ensuring that the children know what they say and how to pronounce all of the words.
- Explain that today the children are going to be the teachers and are going to dictate a sentence to their partner to write.
- Demonstrate turning the sentences face down, choosing one and dictating this to a partner to write.
- Demonstrate checking the sentence using the original sentence as support.
- Remind the children that they need to correct their sentences if there are errors.

5 Review

- Ask the children to remember some of the words that they have been learning this week.
- Display the list of words on the whiteboard for children to use.
- Show the Word art designs from the resources (see You will need).
- Ask the children to use the words to create a 'funky' design in their spelling journals or on paper for display. Encourage them to use fancy writing, colours and to place words in different directions using different sizes.
- Remind the children that they can write the same word several times for effect.

Can you help the kidnapped King's kitten?

Focus: using 'k' for the /k/ sound, as in *sketch, kit, skin*

You will need:

Access online resources at My Rising Stars: www.risingstars-uk.com

- King's Kitten Kidnapped story per pair
- Reminder bubble for display
- Spelling roll playing board per child
- Roll race playing board per child
- Dice and counters
- Soft ball

In a nutshell

Teacher subject knowledge for this unit:

The most common spelling of the /k/ sound is the letter 'c'.
If the next vowel is an 'a', 'o' or 'u' we usually use a letter 'c'.
If the next letter is a 'y' or the next vowel is an 'e' or 'i' we usually use a letter 'k'.
When 'c' is followed by an 'e' or 'i', it makes the soft sound /s/, e.g. *circle, cycle*. If you need the hard sound /ke/ or /ki/ you need to use a 'k'.
If the next letter is a consonant, we nearly always use a letter 'c'.

Word list

sketch	key	skirt
skin	ketchup	skid
kit	kitten	skill
kept	kidnap	frisky

1 Introduce/Review

- Tell the class that this week you are learning the sound 'k' and ask the children to repeat the sound.
- Tell them that there is some very sad news in a newspaper article about the king and you need them to listen very carefully if they are going to have any chance of helping solve a crime.
- Read the article King's Kitten Kidnapped (see You will need) and ask the children to listen out carefully for any words that use the 'k' sound.
- Ask the children if they can remember any of the words that used the 'k' sound.
- Give pairs of children a copy of the article from the resources and ask them to use a highlighter to find all the words that use the 'k' sound as you slowly read it.
- Display the article on the whiteboard and highlight the 'k' sounds with feedback from the class.

2 Teach

- Explain to the children that there are several ways of making the 'k' sound, e.g. *duck, music*.
- Remind the class of the vowels 'a', 'e', 'i', 'o' and 'u'. Explain that when you have an 'e' or an 'i' after the 'k' sound we need to use a letter 'k' rather than a 'c'.
- Show the children the Reminder bubble sheet (see You will need) and leave it displayed for the children to use.
- Demonstrate this with the words *kit, key* and *skin*.

3 Practise

- Display the Reminder bubble from the resources (see You will need).
- Give the children a copy of the Spelling roll resource (see You will need). Tell the children that they need to write one word in each box. All the words that they write should contain the 'k' sound. They should try to use all the words in the word list and each column should contain different words.

Challenge!

Use the Spelling Fox Challenge: Can you help the kidnapped King's kitten? to kick off or consolidate the learning. The children must help the Spelling Fox find the correct answers! Access online via My Rising Stars.

- Explain that by writing the words it will help them practise the spellings and that they will use their completed sheets next lesson.
- Display the word list to support the children in this activity.

4 Apply

Activity 1: Spelling roll

- Give the children their copy of Spelling roll from the 'Practise' session.
- Tell the children that they are going to play 'Spelling roll' using their playing boards.
- Demonstrate how to play the game with a child. Roll the dice and demonstrate that if it lands on number 4 your partner reads out (from your own playing board) the first word in the fourth column for you to write on a whiteboard. Ask your partner to check your spelling using your playing board. If it is correct you can colour in that word on your playing board. (Children could alternatively place a counter over the word they have spelled correctly.)
- Your partner then rolls the dice and you take their playing board ready to read out the relevant word. Remind children to each use a different colour.
- The first person to complete one column on their playing board wins the game.

Activity 2: Roll race!

- Explain that this game is played very much like Activity 1, but in this game it is a race to spell the words correctly.
- This may need demonstrating at the front of the class before the activity begins.
- Give groups of three children the Roll race playing board from the resources (see You will need).
- One child rolls the dice and reads the first uncoloured word in that column number.
- The other two children now race to write the word on their whiteboards correctly first.
- The first child checks the spelling and the child who was first to answer correctly colours in that word on the playing board. The children swap roles and continue, each colouring words that they have won in different colours.
- If the dice is rolled and the column is completely filled then the child can choose to ask any uncoloured word on the board.
- Continue until the board is completely coloured and the child with the most coloured squares wins the game.

5 Review

Activity 3: Quick spell

- Ask the class to stand in a circle.
- Explain that this is a quick game and if the children are not quick they will be out.
- Display the list of 'k' words from the word list on the whiteboard.
- Give a soft ball to a child and ask them to choose a word from the whiteboard, e.g. *kept*.
- The first child throws the ball to another child who says the first letter of the word, e.g. k.
- They throw the ball to another child who says the next letter, e.g. 'e'.
- This continues until a child says the final letter, e.g. 't'. This child throws it one last time to a child who says the whole word, i.e. *kept*.
- Explain that if children are too slow then they will be out and will have to sit down. If the word being spelled out becomes too slow then it may need to be restarted so that it flows clearly.
- Cross out words that have been used so that different words are chosen each time.
- Continue until there are only a few children left standing.
- This game can be repeated several times.